COMMUNICATE!

A Workbook for
Interpersonal Communication

Seventh Edition

Communication Research Associates

Editor-in-Chief
Richard D. Carroll

Author-Editors
Richard D. Carroll
Gregg Florence
Samira Habash
Linda A. Joesting
Betty Martin
Jim Ostach
Dianne G. Van Hook
Roger E. Van Hook
Analisa Ridenour
M. James Warnemunde

Long Beach City College

KENDALL/HUNT PUBLISHING COMPANY
4050 Westmark Drive   Dubuque, Iowa 52002

Book Team

Chairman and Chief Executive Officer   Mark C. Falb
Senior Vice President, College Division   Thomas W. Gantz
Director of National Book Program   Paul B. Carty
Editorial Development Manager   Georgia Botsford
Developmental Editor   Angela Willenbring
Vice President, Production and Manufacturing   Alfred C. Grisanti
Assistant Vice President, Production Services   Christine E. O'Brien
Prepress Editor   Jana Staudt
Permissions Editor   Colleen Zelinsky
Designer   Deb Howes
Managing Editor, College Field   John Coniglio
Senior Editor, College Field   Janice Samuells

ISBN 13: 978-0-7575-1332-9

Printed in the United States of America
10   9   8

SPECIAL ACKNOWLEDGMENTS

We wish to acknowledge the following educators for their years of professional dedication to making *Communicate!* the workbook that it is: Wes Bryan, Herb Caesar, Kat Carroll, Dianne Faieta, Frank Faieta, Lowell Johnson, Molly MacLeod, and Dawn Trickett.

CONTENTS

v

Chapter 6: Understanding Self

Chapter 7: Values

Chapter 8: Managing Conflict

Chapter 9: Relational Communication

Chapter 10: Job Search Skills

Selected Readings   261

Communication Foundations

In this chapter we will explore the different kinds of communication—intrapersonal, interpersonal, and extrapersonal. Communication will be defined, and the term "process" will be explained as it relates to the study of communication.

◈ Process

Definition: When we speak of communication as a process, we are referring to the ongoing, continuous, dynamic sense of relationships existing in all communication. Communication has no beginning and no end.

Example: As I communicate with someone, I send a message to that person. The other person then receives my message and speaks back. As he/she speaks back to me, that person becomes the source and I now become the receiver of his/her message. Throughout the entire communication process, we are constantly changing—changing our roles, changing our language, changing our presentation, changing our attitudes and perceptions.

◈ Communication

General Definitions

- Communication is the process of shared meaning through symbolic interaction. —D. Fabun

- Communication is the process by which we understand others and in turn are understood by them. (It is dynamic, constantly changing in response to the total situation.) —M. Anderson

- Communication involves the conveyance of something to someone else—our ideas, our aims, our wants, our values, our very personalities. —Robinson and Lee

◈ Dyad

A group of two individuals.

◈ **Triad**

A group of three individuals.

◈ **Intrapersonal Communication**

Definition: Intrapersonal communication is the process of communicating with oneself, our self-talk; when we daydream or reflect on what we have done, what is presently going on, or what we will do in the future, we are engaging in intrapersonal communication.

Example: As we consider buying a car, we weigh the pros and cons of one model versus another model in our head before making an overt decision.

◈ **Interpersonal Communication**

Definition: Interpersonal communication is the process of communicating and interacting with other people.

Example: As we are buying a car, we interact with the salesperson, discussing equipment, pricing, financing. We try to work out a deal that is acceptable to both parties.

◈ **Extrapersonal Communication**

Definition: Extrapersonal communication is the process of interacting with beings or articles that are nonhuman.

Example: We can talk to a dog, or a plant, or even yell at our car when it will not start.

THE IMPORTANCE OF COMMUNICATION

Human beings are constantly communicating. In both sending and receiving messages, adults spend almost half of their total verbal communication time as listeners. We spend over one third of our communication time as speakers.

Communication Is a Skill

Because we spend so much time in oral communication, effective communication skills are vital to all of us. Indeed, you may be enrolled in this course to improve your communication skills and to become a more knowledgeable communicator. Employers look for employees who are effective communicators. This course can help you gain these skills.

Communication Links People

During any given day, you may talk to your friends, listen to members of your family, receive correspondence, observe and react to others' gestures and facial expressions, and even carry on conversations with yourself. You, like all humans, are a communicating being. "Communication is the way relationships are created, maintained, and destroyed," observed one communication specialist. Every day, we depend on our abilities to speak, listen, write, read, think, and interpret nonverbal messages. *Without these abilities, we would lose much of what makes us human,* and trying to be human in this very complex world requires all the help we can get. This chapter will show you just how vital communication is to our survival.

Communication Begins Relationships

People often react very differently to the act of getting acquainted, of getting to know someone else. Some people seem to be able to "hit it off" very easily with people they have never met. Other people seem to get sweaty palms, heart palpitations, or nervous stomachs at the very thought of having to meet another person for the first time. Why? We are all human, aren't we? Of course we are, but the answer goes way beyond that.

It is true that in many respects we are all alike; however, we are all unique individuals with different personalities and needs, as well as different levels of socialization skills. The purpose of this text is to help you develop and expand these skills.

BARRIERS TO UNDERSTANDING COMMUNICATION

Communication as a Natural Process

The major barrier to studying intrapersonal, interpersonal and extrapersonal communication is that most people have a tendency to see communication as a **natural process**, requiring little effort or training. After all, we can all talk to a person sitting next to us in this room—can't we? And we seem to make it through life (childhood, adolescence, marriage, relationships, adulthood) interacting with others at each stage—don't we?

The answer to both of these questions is "yes." But wait. True, we may have made it this far in our communicating with others, and could make it the rest of the way through life continuing as we are. The point here is not whether we are "communicating" or not. The real point is whether we are **communicating with maximum effectiveness.** Effective communication is the major concern of this book.

As you study the principles and strategies presented in the following pages, you will begin to see that effective communication is not as simple as most believe. Each chapter presents different barriers that can interfere with communication or prevent effective communication from taking place. You may find, for example, that we do not always really listen to others. Or perhaps we may not describe what we perceive all that accurately. Also, we might not be as aware of ourselves—our values and attitudes or the way we think others see us—as we think. Finally, we might not be handling conflict or our personal relationships as effectively as we could.

Overall, communication requires a great deal of effort to overcome the many barriers that confront us. Our hope is that as you study this essential life skill, the barriers become easier to handle and your relationships with others become more meaningful.

Communication as a Risk

Many people have barriers toward classes such as speech and interpersonal communication. These barriers may have to do with our self-image and with our perceptions of other people.

Self-Image

Self-image barriers include poor self-esteem, shy behavior, lack of social skills, and anxiety over how others may view us. For example, if we have not had much experience in interacting with others in classes, clubs, families, etc., we may be afraid to try. We may be afraid of saying the wrong thing or, if we do speak up, people may not like what we say and thus reject us. Therefore, classes such as this must start with the requirement that we all respect each other, support one another, and refrain from rejecting or judging others.

Perception of Others

Our perception of others can create barriers such as misjudging people, not giving others a chance, and/or stereotyping. For example, if we see someone sitting next to us who has a different hair style or who is from a different racial or ethnic background, we may not want to get to know him or her because of preconceived ideas or beliefs. Stereotypes have no basis in fact—the only thing they do is keep us from getting to know one another. When we get past these barriers and accept people individually, we find that each individual is unique and does not fit these preconceived notions.

TAKE A RISK

We challenge you to *risk* in this class.

- Risk getting to know others.
- Stay open to others and their ideas.
- Do not prejudge others.
- Remember to separate people from their ideas or behaviors.

Others may have different ideas and values from your own but that does not mean that they are not worth knowing.

Again, take risks, keep an open mind, get to know one another, and make new friends in this course.

Communication Questionnaire

PURPOSE

To start you thinking about your views on communication, give you an opportunity to discuss them with other class members, and learn about their views.

PROCEDURE

Complete each of the following statements as openly and honestly as possible. You will then be placed into small groups to discuss your responses and look for things you had in common with the others in your group.

1. When I am around strangers, I:

2. When I communicate with someone, the *hardest* thing for me to do is:

3. When I communicate with someone, the *easiest* thing for me to do is:

4. If I could change one thing about the way I communicate, it would be:

5.   If I could change one thing about the way others communicate, it would be:

6.   In general, most people's communication is:

7.   Communication is / is not important to me because:

8.   Good communicators are people who (*list as many specific behaviors as you can*):

DISCUSSION QUESTIONS

1.   What things did you discover that you had in common with others in your group? How did that make you feel?
2.   What differences did you discover?
3.   Are there any general conclusions you can make regarding what people think or feel about communication? If so, what are they?
4.   How could you act on any of these conclusions to make yourself a better communicator?

Getting to Know Me

PURPOSE

This activity is designed to provide you an opportunity to express some aspects of who you think you are.

PROCEDURE

Complete the following statements with your most honest and immediate reaction. Get into a group and share your responses with one another.

1. I like . . .

2. I'm afraid of . . .

3. Children . . .

4. I hate . . .

5. I wish . . .

6. My life . . .

7. When someone says something I don't like, I . . .

8. Others annoy me when . . .

9. Marriage . . .

10. My ambition is . . .

11. I most regret . . .

12. 1 consider myself . . .

13. When I make a mistake, I . . .

14. My greatest weakness is . . .

15. I think of myself as . . .

16. When things go against me, I . . .

17. I usually get nervous when . . .

18. My friends think that I . . .

19. My greatest joy . . .

20. Few people know that I . . .

DISCUSSION

1. Did you discover any answers you had in common with others?
2. What differences did you discover? Can you account for these?
3. How can sharing this information with a group help improve communication?

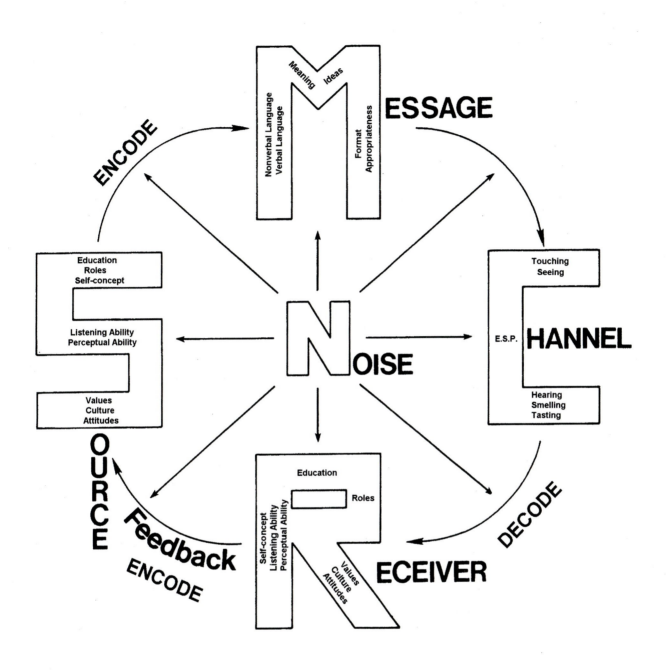

PURPOSE

To consider some basic concepts about communication and to begin thinking about the communication process.

PROCEDURE

Indicate your response to each of the following statements by indicating either **T (True)** or **F (False)**.

True or False

_____ 1. How you communicate has very little impact on what you communicate.

_____ 2. Communication is a natural, human process requiring little or no effort.

_____ 3. When communication is good, both people will understand each other totally.

_____ 4. Dictionaries give us the meanings for most of our words.

_____ 5. We learn who we are from others.

_____ 6. People who talk to themselves are in need of psychiatric help.

_____ 7. Your past experiences and future expectations do not greatly influence your present communication.

_____ 8. Communication basically involves getting our ideas across to others.

_____ 9. Listening and hearing are the same thing.

_____ 10. We can't not communicate.

_____ 11. Most of us perceive the world accurately.

_____ 12. Once we communicate a message, we have no control over what will be done with it.

DISCUSSION

As a class, discuss each question and its implications.

BASIC TERMS

Following are some important terms related to understanding the process of communication.

Basic Communication		
Term	Definition	Example
Source • encoder • speaker	• One who begins communication through verbal or nonverbal means. Other names for source include encoder and speaker.	• Pianist • Instructor
Receiver • decoder • listener • audience	• One to whom the source's verbal/nonverbal communication is directed. Other names for receiver include decoder, listener, audience.	• Audience • Students
Message	• Information or product of the source's purpose, coded into symbols/language and expressed through verbal/nonverbal means.	• Music by Alicia Keys • Lecture-discussion, with visual aids, on why/how we communicate.
Channel • lightwaves • sound/airwaves	• The sense-related medium by which a message is transmitted. Lightwaves, sound, and airwaves are considered as channels.	• Sound/airwaves—sense of hearing, lightwaves—sense of sight.
Feedback	• The receiver's response to the source's message. Feedback indicates how well the source is doing in communicating the message.	• Screams, applause, restlessness at performances; letters afterwards. • Wandering eyes, nervousness, questions, attentive faces during lecture-discussion; good answers on exam afterward.

Basic Communication

Term	Definition	Example
Encoding	• A process involving (1) selecting a means of expression, and (2) transforming ideas into those means through appropriate selection of symbols/language.	• Notes on paper are transformed into music as Alicia plays the piano. • The instuctor selects appropriate language to effectively communicate his ideas.
Decoding	• The receiver's interpretation of the message based on background, education, and future expectations.	• Audience interprets the music according to their capacity. • Students interpret information according to their interest and educational background.
Nonverbal	• The use of hand gestures, posture, eye contact, vocal tone, or personal distance, to emphasize or complement oral communication.	• At the end of each song, the singer raises her arms, stands, faces audience and bows. • When two students are talking in the back row, the instructor stops talking, puts hands on hips and glares in their direction.
Fidelity	• Fidelity is the degree of similarity in meaning between a sender and a receiver. High fidelity communication is the ultimate goal of communication.	• The audience understands the singer's song and begins to identify with its message. • The students understand the instructor's assignment and complete it to everyone's satisfaction.
Mechanical (External) Noise	• Any external interference in the environment that prevents the message from being accurately encoded or decoded.	• A defective microphone screeches through the auditorium. • A loud group walks down the hall. • A police siren blares outside.
Semantic (Internal) Noise	• Any internal interference in one's mind that prevents the message from being accurately encoded or decoded.	• The audience has never heard rock music and has difficulty understanding what it means. • The instuctor refers to concepts the student does not understand.

Defining Communication

PURPOSE

To start you thinking about communication and to determine how much you and the rest of the class already know.

PROCEDURE

The class will be divided into groups and will be asked to discuss the following questions for approximately 30 minutes. Each group should try to reach general agreement on each of the questions. Everyone in the group should be afforded equal opportunities to contribute ideas.

1. What are the major elements of any communication event? (See note below.)
2. Why do you think communication is called a process?
3. What is communication? Describe what you think communication is. Try to arrive at a definition that the group will accept. (Be sure to include the concept of *effective* communication.)
4. What communication barriers did you perceive as your group discussed the above three questions?

DISCUSSION

Record the responses of your group; and be prepared to discuss the conclusion in class.

NOTE

Which of these terms are *absolutely necessary* for communication to occur? These are the elements of communication.

Decoding	Intent	Stimulus
Noise	Understanding	Sender
Listening	Message	Response
Emotions	Process	Encoding
Context	Receiver	Channel
Feedback	Hearing	Transmission

PURPOSE

To analyze and evaluate a variety of definitions of communication.

PROCEDURE

1. Rank the following definitions from 1 to 10.
2. In small groups, compare your decisions with the other members. Explain why you ranked the definitions the way you did. Listen to the other members and see if you understand why they chose their rankings.
3. Each group should pick what the group feels to be the best definition of the 10.
4. Your instructor will then show you how a group of 100 speech "experts" (professionals in the communication field) ranked the 10 definitions at a convention.

Ranking Scale

1 Best
10 Worst

DEFINITIONS OF COMMUNICATION

Rank

_____ A. "In its broadest perspective, communication occurs whenever an individual assigns significance or meaning to an internal or external stimulus."

_____ B. "A communicates B through channel C to D with effect E. Each of these letters is to some extent an unknown and the process can be solved for any one of them or any combination."

_____ C. "Communication means that information is passed from one place to another."

_____ D. "All communication proceeds by means of signs, with which one organism affects the behavior of another (or more generally the state of another)."

_____ E. "The word communication will be used here in a very broad sense to include all of the procedures by which one mind may affect another. This, of course, involves not only written and oral speech but also music, the pictorial arts, the theater, the ballet, and in fact, all behavior."

Rank

_____   F. " . . . the intuitive interpretation of the relatively unconscious assimilation of the ideas and behaviors of one's culture."

_____   G. ". . . the process by which an individual (the communicator) transmits stimuli (usually verbal symbols) to modify the behavior of other individuals (communicates)."

_____   H. "Communication does not refer to verbal, explicit, and intentional transmission of messages alone. . . . The concept of communication would include all those processes by which people influence one another. . . . This definition is based upon the premise that all actions and events have communicative aspects, as soon as they are perceived by a human being; it implies, furthermore, that such perception changes the information which an individual possesses and, therefore, influences him."

_____   I. "This definition (communication is the discriminatory response of an organism to a stimulus) says that communication occurs when some environmental disturbance (the stimulus) impinges on an organism and the organism does something about it (makes a discriminatory response). If the stimulus is ignored by the organism, there has been no communications."

_____   J. "Communication is the assignation of meaningfulness or significance to one's perception of an arbitrary sign."

DISCUSSION

1. Were you surprised by any of the "expert" rankings? Why?
2. Did your group agree that some definitions were better than others?
3. What did the definitions that were ranked near the top have in common?
4. What critical aspects of communication did the bottom-ranked definitions lack?
5. Would it be possible to write a definition of communication that would please everyone who studies it? Why or why not?
6. As you listened to the other group members, could you understand why they ranked the definitions as they did? Why or why not?

Julie and Mr. Conroy

PURPOSE

To examine a communication breakdown and analyze how it could have been prevented.

PROCEDURE

1. Read the following situation.
2. In groups of five to six, answer the questions that follow.
3. Try to achieve consensus as you discuss each item.

"I only figured that any kid who was messing around like that deserved some kind of punishment."

John and Patricia Conroy were apparently no more, no less perplexed by the generation gap than any other parents of a teenage girl. Julie, their 16-year-old daughter, was a good student, reliable, known for her quick smile and friendly manner. She never caused her parents any great problems, though they had long since given up trying to make sense out of the exuberant and slang-filled speech she constantly used.

Julie was an only child, and her parents were often quite restrictive as to where she went and with whom she went. Julie naturally complained occasionally, but there were never any major problems, until one warm June evening.

School had just been dismissed for the summer and Julie was given the family car for the evening to go to a girlfriend's party. She was given careful instructions that she was to be home by 12 o'clock.

The all-girl party was a success, and the happy teenagers were so engrossed in talk that hours slipped by quickly. Someone finally pointed out that it was almost 1 a.m. Julie gasped with surprise and quickly told her hostess that she had to leave. Several of her friends quickly asked for rides home. Julie knew she was already late, so why would a few extra minutes matter?

As she drove down the street toward the first girl's house, one of the other girls in the car spotted two boys she knew walking down the street and asked Julie to stop to give them a ride. Julie knew neither of them but stopped anyway to pick them up. At the next intersection Julie's car was hit broadside by a man who failed to stop at the traffic light. No one was hurt, but the car was inoperable. Police, after questioning all of them, took Julie home in a squad car. Both worried parents came running out of the house to see what happened. In the turmoil of Julie's excited efforts to explain, all her father heard was, "We were riding around with a couple of guys and some old man hit us." Visions of his daughter roaming the streets late at night in a car with boys she didn't even know combined with his built-up tensions, and Mr. Conroy vented his anger by slapping Julie so hard she fell to the pavement. The patrolman attempted to intervene and Mr. Conroy hit him, breaking his nose.

Julie spent 10 days in the hospital with a concussion, the officer needed emergency treatment, and Mr. Conroy was fined $500 and given a suspended sentence for striking an officer of the law. It was months before father and daughter could even begin to talk to each other without anger, and years later, there is still bitterness between them.

DISCUSSION

1. Who was the sender and the receiver of the fateful communication?
2. What effect did the time, place, and circumstances have on Mr. Conroy's action?
3. Did Julie's choice of words have any effect on Mr. Conroy's actions?
4. What effects did the emotions of both Julie and her father have?
5. Were both Julie and her father attempting to communicate? Were they listening to each other?
6. What roles do values play in this incident? What are the possible differences in orientation for Mr. Conroy and Julie?
7. Was the "punishment" by Mr. Conroy related more to what Julie did or what she said?
8. Did Mr. Conroy show any sensitivity to Julie's needs?
9. How could this incident have been prevented?
10. What sort of interference was there in this communication event?

Speech is civilization itself.
The word, even the most contradictory word,
preserves contact. It is silence which isolates.

—T. Mann

Following is a list of 15 problems many individuals have as they try to communicate effectively. Read the list and rank your top five individual concerns.

Ranking Scale

1 = Best
5 = Worst

Rank

_____ A. I often speak before I really think.

_____ B. I usually speak rather than really listen to others.

_____ C. I feel that I am shy.

_____ D. I let others do most of the talking.

_____ E. I would rather communicate in writing than speaking face-to-face.

_____ F. People tell me that I speak too fast.

_____ G. I often misunderstand what people say to me.

_____ H. People often misinterpret what I say.

_____ I. When talking, I gesture more than others.

_____ J. I often interrupt others while they are talking.

_____ K. I feel uncomfortable looking into someone's eyes when talking.

_____ L. When meeting others, I tend to get very nervous.

_____ M. I have trouble when speaking to people in authority positions.

_____ N. I feel that others lose interest in what I am saying.

_____ O. I often find myself playing games with others instead of expressing how I really feel.

DISCUSSION

1. Form a group and compare the things each of you determined that you wanted to work on.
2. Identify those things that you had in common with others. How can knowing that others want to work on the same things help you with your communication?

Course Goals . . .

Following is a list of 15 possible goals and reasons for taking this course. First, read the list and add other goals that might apply to your individual circumstances. Then, select those five goals you feel are most important and rank them.

Ranking Scale

1 = Best
5 = Worst

Rank

_____ A. To organize my thoughts more effectively.

_____ B. To overcome the shyness I experience in talking with people.

_____ C. To communicate more effectively with others.

_____ D. To increase my social skills.

_____ E. To gain confidence in myself.

_____ F. To make myself more marketable for a job.

_____ G. To increase my effectiveness in working in small groups.

_____ H. To increase my vocabulary.

_____ I. To become a better listener.

_____ J. To be more successful in interviews.

_____ K. To speak more clearly.

_____ L. To learn about the various theories of communication.

Rank

_____ M. To become more aware of how I perceive others and how others perceive me.

_____ N. To use my body language/nonverbal communication more effectively.

_____ O. To fulfill my communications requirement.

DISCUSSION

1. Form a group and compare your course goals with one another.
2. Identify those thing that you had in common with others. How can knowing that others may have the same goals help you with accomplishing them?

REACTIONS TO CHAPTER 1

1. What is your personal definition of effective communication?

2. Give three reasons why communication is vital to your survival.

    a.

    b.

    c.

3. Many people feel that communication is an effortless, natural process, requiring little or no work. Do you agree or disagree? Why or why not?

4. Some authorities believe that all communication breakdowns are the fault of the sender. Do you agree or disagree? Why or why not?

5. What does it take for you to open up and disclose yourself to others when you first meet?

Listening

Are you a good listener? Listening is a very important communication skill, yet we seldom receive special training for it in school. People often confuse listening with hearing. Some people play the game of listening by putting on a rubber reaction face along with occasional head nods and verbal sounds.

Listening requires time and effort. It involves much more than hearing. This chapter provides information about listening and activities that will help you learn about this most frequently used element of communication. You must have a desire to apply what you learn if you wish to improve as a receiver.

First, let us understand four very important terms:

◇ Hearing

Definition: Hearing is necessary for listening, but is a separate process involving the reception of sound waves by the ear and brain.

Example: You may hear sounds but not necessarily pay any attention to them. Have you ever been guilty of staring at the speaker when she says, "You're not listening to me"?

◇ Listening

Definition: A mental process of interpreting sound waves in the brain. We focus our hearing upon the stimuli we wish to attend to. Listening isn't passive. You must interpret this stimuli into meaning and action.

Example: Mother, in the kitchen, may be slightly aware of children's laughter and noise coming from the next room, yet can still concentrate on a meaningful task without distraction. But if some unusual sounds occur, they are then interpreted as being significant danger signals.

◇ Empathic Listening

Definition: Listening to discover the sender's point of view. The speaker is encouraged to self-disclose. Establishing trust, the listener enters into that person's world and attempts to imagine the thoughts and feelings of the speaker. Empathic listening responses should be a willingness to understand, but not give advice.

Example: Let us imagine that a fellow student is sharing with a classmate that Professor Jones hates him, is out to get him, and will certainly fail him no matter how hard the student tries. An empathic response might be: "You don't feel Professor Jones is being fair with you?" To suggest that this person is irrational and should "talk it out" with Professor Jones is being judgmental and giving advice.

◇ Feedback

Definition: Those verbal and nonverbal responses that affect the speaker in either a positive or negative way. Feedback may either strengthen or weaken communication. Feedback should express clearly what we want the speaker to know of our understanding about the message.

Example: A student speaker in a public speaking class would be more encouraged upon seeing affirmative head nods regarding a proposal than if he reads anger, negative body language, and glances at the clock.

The Importance of Listening

Most of us have, at one time or another, had the experience of talking with someone and getting the feeling that we weren't being listened to. At such times we may have felt frustrated or perhaps even angry. At other times we may have been in the role of the listener and experienced the embarrassment of being caught not listening. At these times, whether we have been the speaker or the listener, we may have become acutely aware that listening skills, whether someone else's or our own, were not as good as they could or should be. How many times have you made, or heard someone else make, the accusation, "You're not listening to me"? In trying to understand why we are not the listeners we could be, let's consider five questions essential to that understanding:

- How important is listening?
- How good are we as listeners?
- What are the various types of listening?
- What are the major barriers to listening effectively?
- How can we become better listeners?

Listening as a Basic Activity

How important is listening? Beyond our own awareness that it is important to have others listening to us when we are talking, research has indicated that listening is the most used basic communicating activity in our day-to-day lives. On the average, we spend about 70 to 80 percent of our time awake in some kind of communicating. Of that time, we spend approximately 9 percent writing, 16 percent reading, 30 percent speaking, and 45 percent listening. Furthermore, of all the information we come to know during our lifetime, we learn over 90 percent of it through our eyes and ears. In fact, some people have even suggested that the causes of some of the major disasters in history were due to poor listening.

In addition to being the most frequent communicating task that we perform, the importance of listening is further amplified when we consider that listening to someone is a form of recognizing and validating that person's worth. This is probably why we get angry or frustrated, or simply feel rejected when we are not being listened to. How often have you heard, or said, during an argument, "You're not listening to me"? Good, effective listening is a way of reducing hostility, while poor or withheld listening is a way of creating hostility. In fact, intentionally withheld listening has been used as a form of punishment during Victorian times and by primitive tribes. Withholding listening is also a major element in brainwashing techniques. Obviously then, being listened to is a very real need we all have!

Listening as a Skill

Finally, when looking at how important listening is, consider your attitude about people you know who are good listeners. You probably like them more than others who you feel are poor listeners. Research has revealed that being a good listener is considered the most important management skill. So it seems that listening is very important—it's the most used communicating skill. We depend on it heavily for most of the information we come to know. It's important for our success in school, on the job, and in relationships, as well as being vital to our own psychological wellbeing, and it's a key to having more friends.

How good are we as listeners? Listening ability is one communication skill that is relatively easy to measure, and when researchers have measured it, the results have been astounding. Studies have found that the average listening efficiency in this culture is 25 percent. This dismal figure was first discovered in research with college students listening to a 10-minute lecture. While we may wish that the percentage was higher, or even feel that we aren't as bad at listening as other people, the facts suggest that there is a great deal of room for improvement. To test out your own listening efficiency, ask yourself how often you repeat questions that have just previously been answered, ask someone to repeat something she said, write down the wrong information, or try to listen to someone while reading or watching television at the same time. None of us is perfect but when it comes to being a good listener, most of us don't even come close! The logical question to ask is, "Well, if we're such poor listeners, how did we get that way and what's keeping us from being better?" Before dealing with these two questions, let's consider the different kinds of listening that are possible.

Types of Listening

Listening is not just a single activity; rather it is a series of steps relating to a specific goal—what we wish to pay attention to. Just as there is more than one thing to which we can pay attention, there is more than one type of listening. For our purposes, listening can be classified into the following five types:

1. Listening for enjoyment
2. Listening for details
3. Listening for main ideas
4. Listening for overall understanding
5. Listening for emotional undertones

Listening for enjoyment is probably the easiest type of listening we are involved with because, rather than paying attention to someone else, we simply tune into our own emotional response to what we are listening to. This is the type of listening we do when we listen to our favorite radio station or a favorite tune. We enjoy the music for what it does to us, how it makes us feel.

Listening for details is one of the types most closely associated with school. This is the type we use when we are listening for the detailed information in a teacher's lecture. Here we are trying to pay attention to specific factual information that the speaker is trying to relate.

Listening for main ideas is also closely allied with the classroom. However, in this situation we are trying to identify the speaker's main point. What is he driving at? What is the point he is attempting to make? In this type of listening, we must pay more attention and attempt to tune in to the general main ideas.

Listening for overall understanding is even more difficult than the types previously mentioned. In this situation we are trying to piece together all of the speaker's information in an effort to get at the overall meaning in the message. What is the bottom line? In order to do this type of listening, we must attend to much more of the message and try to assemble it in much the same way that a child might assemble a puzzle in order to see the entire picture.

Listening for emotional undertones is yet another type of listening. This is probably the most difficult of all, because it requires the most attention and effort. In this type of listening, we shift our focus from what is being said to how the speaker is *feeling*. We are attempting to understand what is going on inside of her. Unlike listening for enjoyment, where we were concerned with tuning in to our emotions, in this situation we are concerned with the emotions of the other person. This is particularly difficult since emotions are often hidden beneath layer upon layer of verbal camouflage. Often the speaker may not be in touch with her own feelings. Here, great attentiveness to the emotion-laden words is vital along with the discipline to keep our own thoughts and comments quiet.

These, then, are the major types of listening. As we can see, this seemingly simple task is far more complicated than may have previously been thought. But why are we such bad listeners on the average? What keeps us from achieving our goal?

> The word "listen" contains the same letters as the word "silent." —A. Brendel

BARRIERS TO LISTENING

So why are we such bad listeners? While there are probably many causes to poor listening, four major factors can be identified that contribute in large part to the problem.

Physiological Factors

The first major factor is physiological in nature and, as such, is one we must learn to live with: the difference between the thinking and speaking rates. In essence, the brain works much faster than the mouth. Although the average speaking rate in our culture is about 125 words per minute, the brain processes language at the rate of approximately 800 words per minute. Since we can't slow the brain down, this gives us approximately 675 words per minute "free time" in our brain. So how do we use this "free time"? Well, we could use it to reinforce the message we are listening to, or we could use it to identify and organize the speaker's main points and supporting ideas. Unfortunately, most of us use this time to evaluate or criticize the speaker or message, prepare our rebuttal, or just daydream about a million things totally unrelated to the message. In short, we tune in to our own internal dialogue rather than tuning in to the speaker's message.

Some researchers have approached this problem from the other side. If we can't slow down the brain, perhaps we can speed up the message. Speech "compressors," which increase the rate without distorting the tone, have been developed and tested on subjects. Results have shown that it is possible to listen to rates two to three times normal without significant loss of comprehension. In fact, in some instances comprehension has been improved. Perhaps this is due to having less "free time" to allow distractions to creep in and divert the listener's attention. However, even though it sounds promising, "speed listening" is not practical in our day-to-day lives, so we must develop skill that enables us to use this "free time" constructively or we will surely continue to use it destructively.

Psychological Factors

The second major factor for poor listening is psychological. This is the tendency to treat listening as a passive, automatic activity. In other words, we confuse listening with hearing. Hearing is a physical process involving the reception of sound waves. It is passive and automatic. Listening, on the other hand, is an extremely active psychological process requiring attention and interpretation, and involving skills that must be learned. As we have seen, there is more than one kind of listening, and each involves a different set of skills suited to different needs or situations.

When we are actively involved in listening, our blood pressure and pulse rate increase and our palms tend to perspire. We actually burn more calories when we listen. (It might even be possible, but not too practical, to go on a listening diet.) Obviously, therefore, if listening takes work, it is important that we get our bodies ready to work in order to be better listeners, and that we employ the proper skills.

Educational Factors

The third major factor causing poor listening is educational. To understand this factor we must remember two concepts mentioned earlier: listening is the largest part of our daily communication, and listening is an active process. Yet in all the formal education we have received, we have spent major amounts of time learning how to read and write, two skills which total only 25 percent of our daily communication, little if any time learning how to speak in a formal way, and (for the vast majority of us) no time learning how to listen effectively. This is not to suggest reading and writing should not be taught, but when you consider the lack of emphasis that listening skills have received in our formal education, it is no wonder why our average listening efficiency is only 25 percent.

Some private corporations have come to realize the importance of teaching listening skills, and have developed their own listening programs. As the educational community increases its focus on the importance of listening education and more of us are taught proper listening skills, we will hope to see improvement in that 25-percent efficiency rate.

> The reason why we have two ears and one mouth is that we may listen the more and talk the less.
> —*Zeno of Citium*

Social Factors

The last major factor relates to the previous one. Because we have not been taught how to listen effectively, *we often choose the wrong type of listening to do.* Have you ever found yourself tuning in to your own internal dialogue or emotions rather than trying to understand the meaning or emotion in the other person? Have you ever found yourself getting nice and comfortable, as if you were listening for enjoyment, when you were about to listen to a classroom lecture? Clearly, you may have wanted to listen, but you were doing the wrong type of listening.

STEPS TO BETTER LISTENING

How then can we overcome these barriers and improve our listening? As mentioned earlier, listening actually consists of sets of skills that can be employed in different situations to meet different needs. However, there are six steps that actually underlie all the different types of listening skills.

1. **Decide to listen.** Obviously, the commitment to listen is at the heart of being a better listener.

2. **Get your body ready to work.** Remember that listening is work. So it's important to get ready to do work by having an erect posture, being located close to the speaker, and creating some inner tension to combat the tendency to relax and daydream.

3. **Create a supportive climate.** Reduce or eliminate environmental distractions. Avoid statements or actions likely to create defensiveness.

4. **Put the other person first.** Focus on understanding what he/she has to say and use your brain's "free time" to that end.

5. **Select the appropriate type of listening.** Determine what your goal should be and focus on the appropriate part of the other person's message. Is the most important element your own feelings, the other person's details, main ideas, overall meaning, or underlying emotions?

6. **Communicate that you are listening.** Being a better listener is only half the job; you must also let the other person know that you are listening through eye contact, facial expressions, body posture, and feedback.

Because listening is a learned skill, changes won't occur overnight. As with any skill, "practice makes perfect." With the desire to become a better listener, knowledge of listening skills and a willingness to work, major improvements can be made. Then, no one will say to you, "You never listen to me!"

Listening Quiz

PURPOSE

This quiz is designed to get you thinking about the topic of listening, and to expose popular conceptions and misconceptions about listening.

PROCEDURE

To the left of each statement, indicate whether you think that the statement is true or false, by placing a T or F in the blank. Please answer honestly and don't try to "out-guess" the quiz.

True or False

_____ 1. Most people are pretty good listeners.

_____ 2. Listening is an easy, natural, passive behavior.

_____ 3. While listening, it is possible to learn how to pay attention to some other idea, person, event, etc. in our environment at the same time.

_____ 4. There is no way you can "make" someone listen to you.

_____ 5. To be an effective listener we must focus only on what the other person is saying and avoid being distracted by nonverbal cues.

_____ 6. There is basically only one type of listening we can utilize in our day-to-day lives.

_____ 7. When listening to someone with a problem, it's a good idea to offer sympathy or advice when possible.

_____ 8. Good listeners are better liked than bad listeners.

_____ 9. Hearing and listening are essentially the same thing.

_____ 10. Good listeners are born, not made.

_____ 11. Being a better listener simply means taking in more information from the other person.

_____ 12. When we are listening, we are also communicating to the other person at the same time.

_____ 13. To be a really good listener, you have to get inside the other person's head.

True or False

_____ 14. Using feedback is an important part of listening.

_____ 15. Sometimes when listening, the words get in the way.

_____ 16. The single most neglected communication skill is listening.

_____ 17. There are ways to tell when a person is probably not listening.

_____ 18. We spend about 25 percent of our awake time listening.

_____ 19. No matter how good a listener a person may be, he/she will always misunderstand part of what is being communicated.

_____ 20. When people listen to each other more, there is less chance that they will disagree.

_____ 21. The average listening efficiency of this culture is about 60 percent.

_____ 22. Pretending to listen is better than admitting that we're not interested or don't have the time.

_____ 23. The major cause of poor listening is physical rather than psychological.

_____ 24. Good listeners get sweaty palms.

_____ 25. Most people are more interested in "telling their own story" than in listening to anyone else.

DISCUSSION

As a class (or in small groups) discuss each question and its implications.

Listening Skill Exercise

PURPOSE

To practice the "Rogerian" Listening Techniques in order to improve listening skills.

PROCEDURE

1. Form listening triads and designate each participant A, B, or C. In each group, one person will act as referee (observe) and the other two will have a discussion, each alternating between being the listener and the speaker.
2. The discussion is to be unstructured, except that before each participant speaks she must summarize, in her own words and without notes, what the previous speaker said. If the summary is thought to be incorrect, the others are free to interrupt and clarify the misunderstanding. After about seven minutes, the participants switch roles and continue the process. The following topics may be used:

a.	nuclear energy	i.	gun control
b.	Internet regulation	j.	drug abuse
c.	immigration	k.	violence in media
d.	smoker's vs. nonsmoker's rights	l.	abortion
e.	pollution	m.	Education Standards
f.	Affirmative Action	n.	political parties
g.	death penalty	o.	_____
h.	crime/criminals		

Discussion

1. Do we usually listen to all that the other person is saying?
2. Did you find that you had difficulty formulating your own thoughts and listening at the same time?
3. Were you forgetting what you were going to say? Not listening to others? Rehearsing your response?
4. When others paraphrased your remarks, did they do it in a more concise way?
5. How important is it to check out with the other person what you thought you heard her say?
6. Was the other's manner of presentation affecting your listening ability?
7. Does the way another person listens to you affect your self-concept? How?
8. Does the way a person listens to you affect your perception of that person's intelligence and personality? How?
9. What are some guidelines for good listening?

LISTEN

(anonymous)

When I ask you to listen to me and you start giving advice,
you have not done what I asked.
When I ask you to listen to me and you begin to tell me
why I shouldn't feel that way,
you are trampling my feelings.
When I ask you to listen to me and you feel you have to
do something to solve my problems, you have failed me,
strange as that may seem.
So please, just listen and hear me. And if you want to talk,
wait a few minutes for your turn and I promise I'll listen
to you.

It is the providence of knowledge to
speak and it is the privilege of wisdom to listen.
—*O. W. Holmes*

Listening Questionnaire

1. Think about 3 people whom you consider to be good listeners.

   a. What is it about them that makes them good listeners? How do they act, what do they do, what do they say? (Be as specific as possible.)

   b. What is your attitude about these people?

2. Do you consider yourself a good listener? Why/why not?

   a. When do you have the greatest difficulty listening?

   b. When do you have the least?

3. Why would you want to improve your listening?

   a. When do you consider it important for you to listen?

   b. What do you want to gain from studying listening techniques? In what ways do you want to improve your listening? (Be as specific as possible, since these will be your personal objectives for this unit.)

Analysis of My Listening Effectiveness

This form is designed to give you an opportunity to evaluate your own listening effectiveness and for another to evaluate you. Ask another to complete it and return it to you within two days. The information provided will enable you to gain some important insight into your strengths and areas for improvement as a listener.

Part 1—Overall Estimate of my Listening Ability

Please rate my overall ability as a listener according to the following scale:

Poor   Fair   Average   Good   Excellent

Part 2—Assessment of Specific Listening Skills

Section A—For each of the following items, please indicate to the left of each item the frequency with which I demonstrate, to you, the behaviors indicated based upon the following scale:

0	1	2	3	4
never				always

Scale

_____ 1. Appear interested and concerned about what I have to say.

_____ 2. Appear energetic and anxious to listen.

_____ 3. Encourage me to continue communicating.

_____ 4. Indicate if you are confused or don't understand what I am saying.

_____ 5. Respond to what I am saying in a nonevaluative and nonjudgmental way.

_____ 6. Avoid interrupting me while I am speaking.

_____ 7. Look at me when I am speaking to you.

_____ 8. Don't try to change my mind when it's your turn to speak.

Section B—In your own words complete the following two items:

1. What do you consider to be my main strength as a listener?

2. What is the area I most need to work on as a listener?

Listening Skills Self-Inventory

This self-inventory is designed to enable you to assess your skills and behaviors as an effective listener.

PART 1-INITIAL JUDGMENT OF OVERALL LISTENING EFFECTIVENESS

Circle the term below that you feel most closely approximates your overall listening effectiveness:

POOR	FAIR	AVERAGE	GOOD	EXCELLENT
(0)	(38)	(76)	(114)	(152)

PART 2—ASSESSMENT

For each item below, indicate the frequency with which you exhibit that particular behavior according to the following scale:

0	1	2	3	4	5
never					always

Place the appropriate number in the blank to the left of each statement. Be honest in your responses and avoid "out-guessing" the questionnaire.

FRAME OF MIND

Scale

_____ I understand that listening is one of the most important communication skills.

_____ I understand that listening is a major way of "validating" the worth of others.

_____ I am willing to indicate when I don't have the time to listen productively.

_____ I recognize that the goal of effective listening is to understand the other person and her communication as fully as possible.

_____ I treat listening as an "active" skill.

_____ I am willing to listen intently to the other person even though I may disagree with what I think he/she is about to say.

_____ I desire to be empathetic to a person with a problem rather than directing or giving advice.

_____ I recognize that the person with a personal problem is the best one to solve it.

STRATEGIES AND VERBAL BEHAVIORS

Scale

_____ I ask questions to clarify confusion.

_____ I paraphrase what is said to ensure my understanding in vague or especially important areas.

_____ I listen to opposing viewpoints without arguing or defending my own position.

_____ I avoid being distracted by my surroundings or the appearance or mannerisms of the other person.

_____ I begin my conversations with questions rather than statements.

_____ I avoid analyzing the other person while he/she is speaking.

_____ I avoid interrupting the other person.

_____ While listening, I maintain my focus on the other person and what she means by what she says.

_____ I encourage the other person to continue communicating.

_____ I focus my responses on what is said rather than directly on the other person.

_____ I admit that I am confused or unsure when I am.

_____ I try to reduce defensiveness if I perceive that the other person is hostile or angry.

_____ I avoid "invalidating" the other person's emotions and feelings. If he is angry, I acknowledge that he has a right to feel angry.

_____ I avoid asking probing or personal questions.

_____ I avoid giving advice, preaching, or moralizing when listening to someone with a problem.

_____ I avoid collecting "ammunition" for later arguments.

_____ I give honest and assertive responses when they are asked for and when appropriate.

_____ I avoid giving "you should" responses.

_____ I close conversations with a "positive" statement.

_____ I use "I think" or "I feel" when responding about my own reactions.

NONVERBAL BEHAVIOR

Scale

_____ I appear interested by maintaining a pleasant expression on my face.

_____ I look at the other person when he/she is speaking.

_____ I appear unrushed by avoiding "fidgeting," carrying on "standing" conversations, or looking at the clock.

_____ I maintain an "open" posture and level body position.

_____ I appear energetic by using a comfortable but erect and slightly forward-leaning posture.

_____ I maintain appropriate conversational distance by avoiding talking over my desk.

_____ I demonstrate interest, responsiveness and "connectedness" by using head nods, smiles, and vocal responses such as "urn hum," "oh," and "yes" or "yeah."

_____ I "read" the other person's nonverbal cues such as her tone of voice, eye contact, and posture, to enhance my understanding of what she means along with how she feels about what she is saying.

_____ I avoid a relaxed posture that would undercut the effort necessary for effective listening.

_____ I continually monitor the tension in my body that is present when I am working at listening effectively.

TOTAL POINTS FROM PART 2. Compare your total points with the number beneath the word you circled in Part 1.

How does your original estimate compare with your actual score?

Have you discovered any areas you would like to work on?

PURPOSE

To demonstrate how vital listening is to memorization.

PROCEDURE

1. Break into dyads.
2. Have one person in each pair read the following list to the other. The reader should first read item one, then items one and two, and so on through ten. The listener should try to repeat what she heard after each reading.
3. Read the following as directed:
   One pig.
   Two jaws.
   Three orange VWs.
   Four lively pacifiers.
   Five squelching jackasses.
   Six marinated chicks, prepared to perfection.
   Seven fox-trotters from Amazon County, New Delhi.
   Eight rusty outhouse seats unearthed from the tomb of King Tut.
   Nine dirty men, wearing purple tennis shoes, jogging to Lucretia's massage parlor in back of Mr. Yee's gas station.
   Ten amphibious, blubbery octopi legs from the northeast corner of the westernmost island of Mungula-Stikwee, two-stepping to "I Wanna Hug You All Night Long."
4. Get into a circle and see how many can repeat all ten lines.

DISCUSSION

1. What problems did you encounter as you got into this activity? Why?
2. How important is concentration to effective listening?
3. What part can verbal repetition play in acquiring good listening-memory skills?
4. Does the quality of the source's message affect receiver listening?

> **One of the best ways to persuade others
> is with your ears—by listening.** —*D. Rusk*

SUGGESTIONS ABOUT LISTENING HABITS

10 Bad Listening Habits	10 Good Listening Habits
1. Calling subject "uninteresting."	1. Tuning in the speaker to see if there is anything you can use.
2. Criticizing speaker's delivery, personal appearance, etc.	2. Getting the speaker's message, which is probably more important.
3. Getting overexcited and preparing rebuttal.	3. Hearing the person out before you judge her.
4. Listening only for facts.	4. Listening also for main ideas, principles, and concepts.
5. Trying to make an outline of everything you hear.	5. Listening a couple of minutes before taking notes.
6. Faking attention to the speaker.	6. Good listening is not totally relaxed. There is a collection of tensions inside.
7. Tolerating distractions.	7. Doing something about the distractions, closing a door, requesting a person to speak louder, etc.
8. Avoiding difficult material.	8. Learning to listen to difficult material.
9. Letting emotion-laden words affect listening.	9. Trying to understand your reaction to emotion-laden words, which might cause barriers.
10. Wasting difference between speech speed (words per minute) and thought speed (words per minute).	10. Making thought speed an asset instead of a liability by: a. Anticipating the next point to be made. b. Mentally summarizing.

Ralph Nichols and Leonard Stevens, *Are You Listening?*

PURPOSE

To examine your listening habits carefully and identify those that might be improved.

PROCEDURE

Imagine yourself in a classroom or meeting where you are not the most important individual, but a participating member. Score yourself on these 10 worst listening habits:

Rating Scale

1	always guilty
2	almost always
4	frequently
6	infrequently
8	almost never
10	never

Score

_____1. Calling the subject uninteresting. When the subject is a little remote, do you take the first opportunity to "tune out"?

_____2 Reacting to externals. Do you let the speaker's facial expression, accent, or dress interfere?

_____3. Getting overstimulated. Are you easily aroused to anger or unbridled enthusiasm?

_____4. Listening for specifics only. Do you listen to words rather than for themes?

_____5. Writing too little or too much. Do you think you will remember everything without abbreviated notes? Or, equally bad, are you a compulsive note taker?

_____6. Faking attention. Do you smile and nod your head in the speaker's direction? (No extra points for doing it because you think it's polite.)

_____7. Tolerating or creating distractions. Do you let noises outside the room interfere? Do you chat, doodle, play with paper?

_____8. Avoiding difficult material. Are you only attracted to material of general interest?

Score

_____   9. Letting personal prejudice or bias interfere. Do personal biases clog your listening?

_____   10. Wasting the thought-speech ratio. Do you tell yourself you can follow the speech and still do some private blue-skying?

_____   Total Score

Score

90+   Superior
(A psychiatrist or personnel
interviewer might score this high)
80–90   Excellent
70–80   Good
–70   Needs improvement

DISCUSSION

1. Were you surprised by your score? Identify your worst habits and how to improve them.

DILBERT by Scott Adams

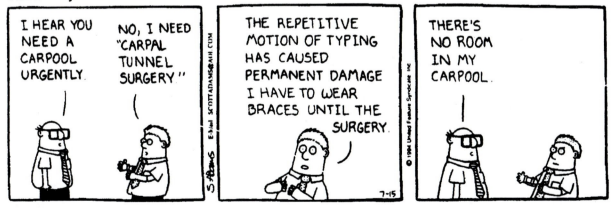

DILBERT reprinted by permission of United Feature Syndicate, Inc.

Active Listening

PURPOSE

To increase your active listening skills.

PROCEDURE

1. The first part is based on programmed instruction. Simply read and follow each step.
2. After completing the programmed section, role-play the situations suggested in the "Active Listening Exercise."
3. Try to determine the extent to which active listening is used in each of these situations.
4. Cover all sections, except 1, with a sheet of paper

1. This program is designed to help improve communication between people. You should be covering all of this page so that only this first instruction is exposed. Each printed instruction is called a frame. A black line, like the one below, means the end of a frame. After you have finished reading this frame, move the cover down to the black line below the next frame.

---

2. There are several reasons for attempting to improve communication. For one thing, in any relationship that the partners want to develop, situations will appear in which one person wants to talk about a problem and the other wants to listen. This session focuses on an approach to listening.

---

3. Experience has shown that people who work with others in solving problems typically go through specific stages of relating. At each stage they require new, more useful ways of looking at their problems, which leads them to better understanding and to new approaches to solutions. These new approaches come from changes in their awareness, thinking, feeling, and doing.

---

4. This program focuses on the first stage of relating to one another, that is, actively listening to the other so he can freely explore with you what is on HIS mind.

5. This is a step-by-step learning program. You will be learning from a series of brief exercises that involve YOU in DOING something. You will be learning from *your own experience*.

6. Now we can begin. I am going to describe an incident to you that involves you and another person in conversation. It ends with the other replying to you and waiting for your response. I will then give five possible responses. Imagine you are listening to the responses. Then read below and pick the ONE that is most likely to encourage the other to keep telling you what's on HIS mind, and to help you both explore the problem as HE sees it.

7. Here's the situation: A person in your class is telling you about how hard it has been lately for him to do the homework. You ask him why and he replies, "I don't know why, I just can't get to it. Frankly, I don't have any enthusiasm for doing it. I've lost interest in the class. I just stall around and then rush like mad to even get here on time every day."

8. Which of the following responses is most likely to encourage the other to keep talking about what's on his mind and what he is feeling?
    a. Don't you know that you are not going to get anything out of the class if you don't do your homework?
    b. You've just got to get it done or you'll flunk.
    c. What's happening? You been playing around too much?
    d. You shouldn't be late so much. It's not fair to the rest of us.
    e. It sounds as though you've lost your enthusiasm and interest in the class.

9. Write your answer here

10. Now let's continue. We will go through more steps before I tell you the answer I would give. It is not important whether your answer and mine agree; however, it IS important that you understand my answer. The purpose of the next few steps is to develop that understanding.

11. Now let's look at what the other is feeling. Pretend to be the other and speak his words aloud and with feeling. How do you feel as you speak the other's words? "I don't know why. I just can't get to it. Frankly, I don't have any enthusiasm for doing it. I've lost interest in the class. I just stall around and then rush like mad to even get here on time every day."

_____

12. Write down some of your feelings as you spoke. Were you happy or sad? Were you angry? Write your feelings in the next frame.

_____

13. 1 felt:

_____

14. Many people report feeling discouraged, depressed, down, bummed out, dull, bored, listless, aimless, etc. Were the feelings you had generally the same, or were they different? (If your feelings were quite different, listen to the words again and try to feel them as having a discouraged, aimless feeling. The fact that you felt differently does not mean you were wrong, but that you just felt differently.)

_____

15. The first possible response was: "Don't you know that you are not going to get anything out of the class if you don't do your homework?" Imagine that you are the other and are lacking in enthusiasm and have lost interest in your class. How do you feel when you hear this response? Write some of your feelings in the space below.

_____

16. 1 felt:

17. Some people feel blamed, punished, criticized, resentful, misunderstood, annoyed, angry, etc. Other people feel blamed, regretful, bad, hurt, apologetic, sorry, etc. Were your feelings close to any of those?

_____

18. Now react to each of the other responses as if you are the other. Remember that you have said: "I don't know why. I just can't get to it. Frankly, I don't have any enthusiasm for doing it. I've lost interest in the class. I just stall around and rush like mad to even get here on time every day."

_____

19. Speaker's response to you: Your reaction to the speaker:

    a.   a.

    b.   b.

    c.   c.

    d.   d.

    e.   e.

_____

20. In looking back over your reaction, remember that *what a speaker intends or means to say* does not necessarily affect a listener's feelings. The listener's feelings are affected by what he **hears** the speaker saying. With that point in mind, revise what you have written if you want to.

_____

21. In our incident, the **other's** personal feelings are probably strong during the early part of this conversation and almost any response will move him AWAY from expressing what's on HIS mind. He may move away because he feels you are blaming, criticizing, or analyzing him. Even if you are supporting or approving, he is likely to move away from freely exploring what's on HIS mind, because he wants to keep getting the good feeling of your support and approval.

22. Now let's think about some different ways of responding to another person. The ones given in the exercise are evaluating, forcing, probing, directing, and accepting.

23. Each of the five responses you were given earlier is an example of a different way of responding by the respondent (R) to the speaker (S).

Response "a" says: "Don't you know that you are not going to get anything out of this class if you don't do your homework?"
These words are FORCING. They begin with "Don't you . . ." and the rest of the words express R's opinion about what S is doing. Look at the words again. The question FORCES S into agreeing with R's opinion and leaves S free only to admit that he "knows" or "doesn't know" that he's "letting himself down." The question shifts S's attention to what is on R's mind.

Response "b" says: "You've just got to get it done or you'll flunk."
These words are DIRECTING. They *tell* the other to *do* something. They also shift S's attention on what R considers important or interesting.

Response "c" says: "What's happening? You been playing around too much?"
These words are PROBING. They *ask for information* about a hunch the responder has. They focus S's attention on what R considers important or interesting.

Response "d" says: "You shouldn't be late so much. It's not fair to the rest of us."
These words are EVALUATING. They place blame on the other for the practice of unfairness.

Response "e" says: "It sounds as though you've lost your enthusiasm and interest in the class."
These words are ACCEPTING. They repeat the other's *key words* back to him without judging him. S knows that he has been heard and he is free to keep talking about what's on his mind.

---

24. In my experience, the response that is most likely to encourage the OTHER to keep telling you what's on HIS mind and to help you both explore the problem as HE sees it is the **accepting** response (e).

---

25. Later in a conversation, other kinds of responses can be helpful in (1) exploring the facts and feelings that are not at the surface of the other's mind, (2) in creating alternative solutions, (3) in evaluating alternatives, (4) in deciding, and (5) in motivating action.

26. Until the other gets **his feelings** off his chest and really feels you have understood and accepted his feelings, his communication will contain facts distorted by his feelings. Until you actively show your understanding and acceptance of his feelings, it is too soon for you to explore facts, create alternative solutions, or suggest action.

---

27. There is a logical sequence in working with another person to **solve a problem.**

ACCEPTING and UNDERSTANDING the other's way of seeing and feeling about things as being HIS, then
EXPLORING and PROBING for facts and feelings, then
CREATING alternative solutions, then
DECIDING on one solution, then
ACTING, then
FOLLOWING UP to see what is happening, . . . ETC.

This session focuses on the first step—developing your ability to respond in an **ACCEPTING** way when you feel it is appropriate.

---

28. Now we will look at another incident. A student in your class seems to be unable to do the work, and tells you, "I just can't seem to get the hang of things. I try to find out what I'm supposed to do on tells me. No one pays attention to me and I can't learn anything by just watching. Maybe I ought to quit."

---

29. Which of these responses is *accepting?*
   a.   "Why don't you try harder? No one gets ahead without hard work."
   b.   "If I were you, I'd ask the other people to help you."
   c.   "Do you have any ideas why the others won't help you?"
   d.   "Don't feel too bad. All of us have problems."
   e.   "You feel that the others don't pay attention to you?"

---

30. Answer "e" is *accepting.* It reflects the other's main thinking and feelings.

---

31. Here's another incident. A student tells you, "That teacher! I've been here three years and no one ever told me before that I did a lousy job. So I made a few mistakes, but why does she blame me for everything?"

32. Which response is *accepting?*
    a. "All she wanted to do was to get you to be more thorough."
    b. "You think she expects too much of you?"
    c. "She really doesn't blame you for everything. She just wanted you to do it over again."
    d. "You feel she blames you for everything."
    e. "Are you really sure it's not all in your mind?"

---

33. Response "D" is *accepting.* It reflects the other's main thinking and feelings.

---

34. This time, you do the responding yourself. I'm going to say something to you and you will then write down an *accepting* response in the following frame.

---

35. I say, "I don't usually admit it, but I often have feelings of inadequacy when I'm asked to speak before a group of people. I'm sure they think I don't know what I'm talking about because I get so shaky and lose my train of thought."

---

36. You respond:

---

37. Now imagine that you are the person speaking. You have just said, "I don't usually admit it, but I often have feelings of inadequacy when I'm asked to speak before a group of people. I'm sure they think I don't know what I'm talking about because I get so shaky and lose my train of thought." Now listen to 10 possible responses. *Put a check in front of the responses that are **accepting** to you.*

    a. "You get shaky when you speak before a group?"
    b. "How do you know what the group thinks about you?"
    c. "Don't you realize that even the best speakers get a little shaky?"
    d. "When did this kind of thing first happen to you?"
    e. "Why are you afraid to admit to such a minor neurosis?"
    f. "You feel inadequate and lose your train of thought?"
    g. "I've had the experience many times. Have you tried taking deep breaths?"
    h. "Do you think this inferiority complex stems from your early childhood?"
    i. "Don't you think that this will hurt you in your activities as a leader?"
    j. "Wouldn't you like to sit in on the 'Speaking in Meetings' course I'm taking?"

38. Responses "a" and "f" are **accepting.**

---

39. Take a minute to look back at the responses you wrote down. Do they still seem accepting?

---

40. Now listen to a series of expressions. In the right hand column, write an *accepting* response.

Others say: *You say:*

"I don't think you understand some of the problems with this assignment."

"Sure I want to improve, but I think I'm doing all I can right now. After all, if I take time out to go to the lab sessions, my job will suffer."

"Do you really think I don't take enough initiative? I've always prided myself on my ability to really plunge into an assignment."

"I think you've got a fine idea there; however, I really doubt that the teacher will buy it."

(ANGRY) . . . "Most of the people in this class don't give a damn about it, so why should I?"

---

41. Some *accepting* responses that you might give to the aforementioned expressions are:

   a. "I don't understand some of the problems with this assignment." (And yet, I might say this with a tone of voice that says, "That's what YOU think, but I really DO understand." If I do say it this way, however, the other still won't feel understood or accepted.)
   b. "You want to improve but your work will suffer if you go to the study sessions."

c. "You feel that you really plunge into an assignment but I think you don't take enough initiative." (I would need to reassure him that I didn't see him. However, if I do reassure him, then I stop his talking about what is on HIS Mind.)

d. "You doubt that the teacher will buy it." (I would feel a need to start telling him how he could get the teacher to buy it. It might be that this is not the main thing on his mind. I won't find THAT out, though, unless I hear him out.)

e. "Why should YOU care when most of the people in this class don't give a damn about it." (I am just repeating his idea—not asking a question.)

---

42. Review your responses in frame 40 and revise them if you want to. As you revise them, think about the tone of voice in which you would say them. Think about how the other would react to your tone.

---

43. Experiment with ACCEPTING responses in your encounters with people for the next few days, and try to sense how people react. The only way to develop the skill of **accepting** is through practice. When you are really tuned into the other's world, you will find (if your experience is like mine) that the other becomes noticeably more interested in talking to you. YOU will enjoy it more, too.

---

44. a. As you listen, your main purpose is to ACTIVELY show the other that you are "with him," "in tune," "understanding him," and "caring about what he is trying to communicate to you." (If you don't honestly care, that will show through and the **accepting** responses will sound phony.)

b. You can show that you are "in tune" in other ways than accepting words. For example, there are times when the most helpful thing you can do is to be **quietly attentive.** Nodding your head, to let the other know you are with him, can help, too.

c. As the other continues talking to you, do more than just parrot his words. Try to capture the flavor of his ideas and his feelings, that is, try to be a mirror. If you are a clear mirror (and not a "judge" or a "critic"), he will feel free to change with you and in front of you. (And, if your experience is like mine, that can be a very satisfying experience.)

---

45. The next frame lists several statements. Try thinking of responses that catch the flavor or spirit of what the other is saying without just being repetitious of his words. Write your responses in the right hand column of the next frame.

46. *Others say:*   *You say:*

"It really gripes me when people say
that. Ever since I was a kid in
elementary school people have said I
was stubborn. I'll be damned if I can
see how being a 'wet mop' will help
me to do a better job!"

(INCREDULOUSLY) . . . "You
mean somebody said that about me?"

(ANGRY) . . . "One trouble with
people in our class is that they never
can see that we need answers now. I
think too many of you have been
concentrating on theories that still
need to be proved."

"I doubt that it will work. I don't
think you understand our problem.
Our situation is completely different
from anyone else's."

"It's hard to say where I would like to
be five years from now. I certainly
would like, gee . . . I don't know. I
feel I could be doing a lot more than I
am . . .; but, somehow, it doesn't seem
worth it. Why bother trying?"

---

47. Answers I might give are:

   a.   "It really gripes you when people call you stubborn."
   b.   "You are surprised to hear that."
   c.   "You are angry that we don't get answers for you right away."
   d.   "You feel that I don't understand your situation."
   e.   "Are you saying that life seems pretty overwhelming to you? That you feel
        like you'd like to do something—but why bother?"

---

48. As you practice using accepting responses, you may feel discomfort. If you do,
    remember that a new way of behaving is usually uncomfortable at first.

DISCUSSION QUESTIONS

1. When do you think Active Listening should be used?
2. Has anyone ever done this kind of listening with you? If so, how did it make you feel?
3. Since Active Listening is a skill and must be practiced to improve it, how do you think you could practice Active Listening?

Active Listening Exercise

PURPOSE

To practice creating Active Listening responses.

PROCEDURE

In small groups, discuss each of the following statements. What responses should be made? Why? If Active Listening is called for, suggest an appropriate Active Listening response.

1. I wonder if I ought to start looking for another job. They're reorganizing the company, and what with the drop in business and all, maybe this is one of the jobs they'll cut back on. But if my boss finds out I'm looking around, maybe he'll think I don't like it here and let me go anyway.

2. I said I'd do the collecting for him, but I sure don't feel like it. But I owe him a favor, so I guess I'll have to do it.

3. I've got a report due tomorrow, an exam the next day, rehearsals every night this week, and now a meeting this afternoon. I don't think I can even fit in eating and this has been going on all month.

4. Sure she gets better grades than I do. She's a housewife, takes only two classes, and all she has to do is study. I have to work a job and go to school too. And I don't have anyone to support me.

5. I can't understand why they haven't written. They've never been gone this long without at least a card, and I don't even know how to get in touch with them.

6. My daughter got straight A's this year and the high school has a reputation for being very hard. She's a natural student. But sometimes I wonder if she isn't all books. I wish I could help her get interested in something besides studying.

7. I worked up that whole study—did all the surveying, the compiling, and the writing. It was my idea in the first place. But he turned it into the head office, with his name on it, and he got the credit.

8. Boy, the teacher tells us he'll mark us off on our grade every time we're late, but it doesn't seem to bother him when he comes in late. He must figure it's his privilege.

9. I don't know whether I'm doing a good job or not. She never tells me if I'm doing well or need to work harder. I sure hope she likes my work.

10. She believed everything he said about me. She wouldn't even listen to my side; she just started yelling at me.

11. Look, we've gone over and over this. The meeting could have been over an hour ago if we hadn't gotten hung up on this one point. If we can't make a decision, let's table it and move on.

12. Look, I know I acted like a rat. I apologized, and I'm trying to make up for it. I can't do anymore, can I? So drop it!

DISCUSSION

1. Did your groups have difficulty in developing Active Listening responses?
2. Did the groups have any difficulty with responses to #6 and #12? Why?

REACTIONS TO CHAPTER 2

1. Why is listening such an important communicating skill?

2. Why is it that we have a tendency to evaluate what a person says rather than listening with understanding?

3. Explain why we don't need training to hear, but we do need training to become better listeners.

4. What kinds of verbal and nonverbal feedback can we use to let a person know we are listening?

5. Select a specific listening experience where you blocked out what the person was saying. What are some ways you plan to overcome this bad listening habit?

6. Where do you plan to practice empathic or active listening? How do you expect it to improve your communication?

Perception

We spend our entire lives communicating our perceptions of what we think our world is like, what is happening in it and what we are doing about it.

Thus, what and how we perceive constitute critical elements in our study of communication.

◈ Perception

Definitions:

- The manner in which we assign meaning, value, significance, and usefulness to elements in our environment

- The sensing, processing, organizing, and interpreting of our reality

Examples:

Consider the following situations. Your *perception of* the central figure in each will determine your *reaction to* it.

As you are casually strolling through your own neighborhood, you observe a female black kitten on the sidewalk in front of you. Do you:

- Want to lift, cuddle, and talk to her because she is soft, loving and vulnerable?

- Step around but otherwise ignore her because you are simply not interested in cats?

- Avoid even looking at her, crossing to the other side of the street, because in your mind she is associated with the devil and bad luck?

As you continue through this chapter, you will become more aware of the importance of perception in everyday communication.

THE IMPORTANCE OF PERCEPTUAL AWARENESS

If you were in a shoe store and asked the sales person for a pair of black cowboy boots in size 8, and the individual returned with a pair of calf-skin loafers in size 9, you might think that the salesperson was not listening. It may be that he did hear you but flashed on calfskin when you said cowboy, perceived you as preferring loafers, and thought that a size 9 might be a more comfortable fit for you. This kind of misperception occurs often in our interactions with others. It happens because we think that everyone sees the world the same way that we do. But they don't. Just as each of us has different fingerprints or a unique voice print, a person's perceptions likewise carry a unique code. We will examine four key factors that are responsible for our individual perceptions of the world. These four factors determine how we select, organize and interpret our experiences into a meaningful picture of the world around us.

The Four P's of Perception

Effective communication skills can help us bridge our innate differences. But, we can only share perceptions in so far as we are able to see the other person's perspective. When we communicate we share our *perception* of the world, not necessarily the *truth*. Some reasons for the differences in the perceptual process include:

- physiological factors
- psychological factors
- position in space
- past experiences

Taking each of the four in turn, it is interesting to consider the odds against effective communication.

Physiological factors include what we are able to perceive, that is, what capacity we possess with our senses of sight, touch, hearing, taste and smell. You might try wearing someone else's eye glasses just long enough to experience how different that person's world must appear to him or her. Compound that difference by putting cotton in your ears to reduce your ability to hear, or wear cotton gloves to reduce sensitivity of your touch. You might notice how different the world appears if you wear a 25-pound weight belt around all day. It is difficult to imagine that the world that we experience is not the same world that every other person experiences.

Psychological factors encompass what we need to perceive and, therefore, do. We all differ in immediate needs, desires, interests, and motives. Thus, we tend to pay attention to only—or especially—those things which interest us. The continual barrage of external stimuli necessitates that we attend to limited aspects of our environment; however, we make choices not randomly but with our psychological drives as a primary motive. For example, two friends are riding together in a car. If one is looking for entertainment or a good time, he is more likely to see the theaters and bars; the other, who happens to be tired after a long day at work, may fail to see any of those. The less energetic of the two may, in fact, tend to focus on relaxation-oriented stimuli. Most of us are so good at paying attention only to what interests us that we even distort external events and things to make them fit what we want to perceive. The need for beauty, for example, can be strong enough that someone can find it in rubble. An intense need for security may cause someone to sense trouble where it does not exist. An unsatisfied need for love or friendship might cause one to recognize a reciprocal desire in another person where it may not merit this perception.

Position in space of a person certainly adjusts what can be seen. We are limited in what we perceive by angle, height, and location in time and space. How different a parade must appear to a small child perched on her dad's shoulders, compared to a little boy standing on the ground.

Past experience is our last stop in this sequence of P's. People tend to perceive according to what they've learned to perceive. Call it expectation or even anticipation, but regardless of terminology, it is the knee jerk of familiarity. Our familiarity with something helps us to accept it as well as recognize it. Our past experiences accompany us in each perception we have.

Cue Sensitivity

The P's of Perception are four in number; the cues are innumerable. Cue sensitivity is still another way of understanding the selectivity of perception. The cues are external to oneself out there in the world of stimuli; the sensitivity is internal and quite individualized. The sensitivity or lack of it on the part of the individual is not uniform or equivalent by any stretch of the imagination. The following list indicates some reasons why we might overlook some of the cues that exist.

- *Familiarity.* We often ignore what we take for granted. The "a's" and "the's" on this page were probably not even seen by you, yet they are indeed printed. A gate passed through daily is not there consciously. A frequently heard sound disappears, but only in your perception. A spouse's repeated question is simply not heard. Such cues may not seem important until demand or change forces recognition—bringing with it a degree of consequence, too *often* negative in nature.

- *Complacency.* Our very contentment can serve to disarm us and render lessened degrees of sensitivity. A relaxed state of body and/or mind can diminish our awareness. Trained states of relaxed awareness such as meditation can overcome this; however, on a daily scale of activity we become numb as our needs are satisfied.

- *Lack of experience or knowledge.* If something is not familiar at all, a signal for danger for example, no capacity for sensitivity is yet developed for one's own protection. A child soon learns the hazard of a hot stove. Any noise, smell, or sight is not an understood cue for the untried perceiver. New ideas or values could be included here also.

- **Problem Paralysis.** The person who is experiencing problem overload or sensory overkill and is burdened from within is likely to miss that which is outside. There simply is no room for one more thing.

- **Singularity.** Thoughts or concerns that are near-obsessive tend to override other stimuli. The task-oriented, Type A personality attempting to succeed in a given assignment may block not only distractions but also helpful cues as well. Many generals have, indeed, won the battle but lost the war.

Having examined cue sensitivity from the standpoint of reasons for overlooking important cues, a brief summary of why we see particular cues might be illuminating. Our degree of awareness—our internal sensitivity—stems from knowledge, sensing selectivity, vigilance, vocabulary, topic interest, open-mindedness, experience, and even practice.

Because of the P's and cues, we tend to individually select from a myriad of cues, organize in a way that makes sense to us, and interpret based on our unique experiences. It is important to keep in mind that no one else sees the same world that we see.

BARRIERS TO PERCEPTION

Let's summarize some of the problems we have communicating with others because of our perceptions. We tend to perceive the world in terms of our own needs, wants, experiences, culture, expectations and physical abilities or limitations regardless of what external reality might be. Because our perception process is unique to each of us, we often perceive the world very differently from those around us.

We have trouble communicating with others when we fail to be aware that we perceive the external world through our senses (an internal process) and we can be fooled. Even the symbols (both verbal and nonverbal) we use to communicate our perceptions to others may have meanings which are considerably different from what we intend our receiver to understand.

The Perceptual Process

The perceptual process can cause confusion about what is going on in the real world. We believe what we perceive; we treat it as truth. On the other hand, another person with whom we are communicating believes that what he/she perceives is what is going on in the real world and treats it as truth. What is it about the perceptual process that allows such unique selectivity to occur?

- **We believe that our world of experience has structure.**

The question here is: how do our senses interact with the real world? Many people assume that our eyes, ears, nose, and fingers impassively connect with the world the way a video camera does—passively. If that were the case, our senses would record everything that was happening to us and then we would sort it out at the cognitive level. That is, we would interpret it later. What actually happens is that the very act of sensing is also one of creating. We perceive the world that we are prepared to perceive. An example can be seen by doing a little experiment. Use figure 3.1. Have one or more people first look only at drawing (a), then have one or more people look only at drawing (c). Then have all of the people look at drawing (b) and ask them if they see the old lady or the young lady.

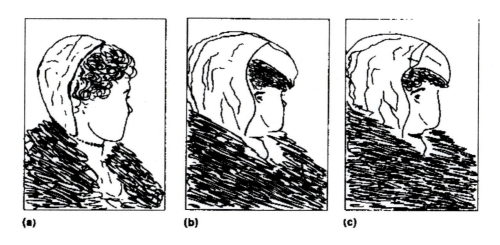

Fig. 3.1. Perception.

Chances are, they will see the person similar to the one that they saw first. The people whom you asked to look at the pictures had been preconditioned to process the input stimuli in a certain way, and they created a structure consistent with that mind-set. In this categorizing process, a person extracts stimuli from the world and forces that stimuli into a set of categories. The categories we use are derived from our past history, so for each of us we create a world of structure.

• Our world of experience has stability.

When we open our eyes and look at a scene, we are not aware of the constant shifts in the picture as our eyes and our attention wander. There is an enduring aspect to our experience. We select certain facets of the situation and stick with them. Check this statement against your own experience with the ambiguous picture in figure 3.1. If it was like the experience of most people, your first perception of the picture, whether it was the old lady or the young woman, continued to demand your attention. In order to understand the world we experience, it is easier for us to give it stability.

• Our world of experience is meaningful.

Can you conceive of a world in which everything was random, with no apparent causal relationships? Nothing would seem familiar. The general experience would be one of chaos. Such a state of affairs is so alien to our everyday life experience that it is extremely difficult to imagine.

We make our experiences meaningful so that they are related and seem familiar. In a way, that is what we do when we look at a cloud in the sky and imagine that it is an elephant or a rabbit. We constantly do this with every aspect of our daily lives. We force two or more nonrelated events into a meaningful relationship. And we do it differently from anyone else. This means that everyone else will create a different meaning from life experiences.

In order to give the world of our perceptions structure, stability, and meaning, we must organize it. The way we do this causes our perceptions to differ from everyone else's.

Perception: Agree/Disagree

PURPOSE

To test your understanding of basic perception principles.

PROCEDURE

1. Read each statement carefully.
2. If you believe it to be true, check the Agree column under Individual. If you believe it, or any part of it, to be false, check the Disagree column under Individual.
3. For each of the following statements, check if you agree or disagree.

| Individual | | | Group | |
Agree	Disagree		Agree	Disagree
		1. The perception of a physical object or event depends more upon the object or event than upon the mind of the observer.		
		2. Perception is primarily an interpersonal phenomenon.		
		3. The fact that hallucinations and dreams may seem as real as waking perception indicates that perception depends very little upon external reality.		
		4. The reaction we have to what we see generally depends upon learning and culture.		

Individual			Group	
Agree	Disagree		Agree	Disagree
		5. We tend to see what we wish to see or are expecting to see regardless of what reality is.		
		6. We can eliminate all distortion in our perception by careful, scientific observation.		
		7. Scientific instruments, though they extend the limits of our perception, do not make perception any more real.		
		8. What we perceive is no more than a representation of what is.		
		9. Perception is a physical response to a physical reality. It is only when we begin talking about our perceptions that we begin to distort them.		
		10. If we are careful, we can see the world as it really is.		
		11. We react to our environment on the basis of what we perceive that environment to be like and not on what the environment is really like.		

DISCUSSION

Your instructor will lead a discussion, comparing Individual and Group responses.

PURPOSE

This model exercise allows you to become aware of several variables that contribute to the formation of a perception.

PROCEDURE

1. This activity mat be done individually, or in small or large groups.
2. Select (or you may be assigned) a "real life" situtation (e.g. education, premarital sex, homelessness, gender roles).
3. Use the terms in the wheel to review your feelings, values, judgments, and opinions of the assigned situation.

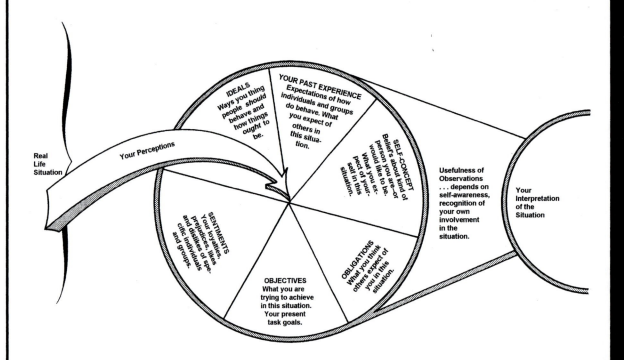

Factors affecting your interpretation of a situation.

Dr. Robert L. Katz, *Developing Human Skill*; © 1955, Amos Tuck School of Business Administration, Dartmouth College.

Rorschach ink-blot
What do you perceive?

"Black Signature" by Magritte
What do you perceive?

What do you perceive?

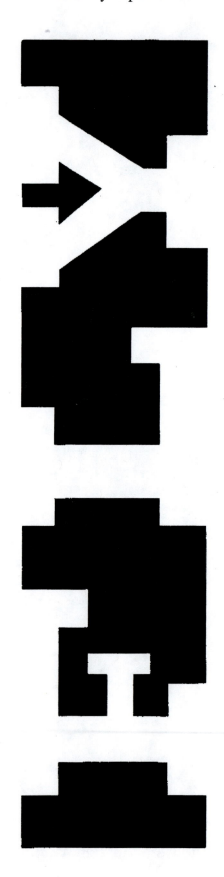

What do you perceive?

Check Your Perception

PURPOSE

To give you a chance to check your perception.

PROCEDURE

1. Read the following aloud.

Paris in the the Springtime	Bird in the the Hand	Once in a a lifetime

2. How many times does the letter F appear in the box below?

> FINISHED FILES ARE THE RESULT
> OF YEARS OF SCIENTIFIC STUDY
> COMBINED WITH THE EXPERIENCE
> OF MANY YEARS

What do you perceive?

What do you perceive?

From *Hidden Dimensions* by Dan Dyckman, copyright © 1994 by Dan Dyckman. Used by permission of Harmony Books, a division of Random House, Inc.

The Author at Work
What do you perceive?

PURPOSE

To determine how accurately we perceive our commonplace world.

PROCEDURE 👤

This is a timed test. You have 10 minutes. Place your answer to the left of the number; you are encouraged to guess.

_____1. On a standard traffic light, is the green on the top or the bottom?

_____2. In which hand is the Statue of Liberty's torch?

_____3. Name five colors in the Campbell's standard soup label?

_____4. What two digits on a standard telephone dial are not accompanied by letters?

_____5. How many wieners in a standard package?

_____6. When you walk, does your right arm swing with your right leg or your left leg?

_____7. How many matches are in a standard pack?

_____8. On the American flag, is the uppermost stripe red or white?

_____9. Does the writing on a pen or pencil run from point to end or end to point? (Don't cheat)

_____10. What is the lowest number on an FM radio dial?

_____11. On a standard computer keyboard, over which number is the "%" (percent) symbol?

_____12. Which way does the water go down the drain in the northern hemisphere—clockwise or counter-clockwise?

_____13. Which side of a woman's blouse has the button holes?

_____14. Which way does the red diagonal slash go in the international "no parking" or "no smoking" signs?

_____15. How many channels are on a standard VHF (commercial) television tuner?

_____16. What four words appear on every denomination of U.S. coin and currency?

_____17. Which direction do the blades of a fan rotate (as it blows on you)?

_____18. Whose face is on a dime?

_____19. How many sides does a stop sign have?

_____20. Do books have their even-numbered pages on the left or right?

_____21. What is the room number of this classroom?

_____22. How many lug nuts are on a standard-sized American car wheel?

_____23. How many hot dog buns in a standard package?

_____24. On which card in the deck is the card maker's trademark?

_____25. On which side of a standard mini blind is the rod that adjusts the opening between the slats?

_____26. On the back of a $5 bill is the Lincoln Memorial. What is in the center of the back side of a $1 bill?

_____27. How many sides are there on a standard pencil?

_____28. Does a carousel turn clockwise or counter-clockwise?

_____29. How many curves in a standard paper clip?

_____30. Sleepy, Happy, Sneezy, Grumpy, Dopey, and Doc. Name the seventh dwarf.

Score

28–30 Excellent
25–27 Good
20–24 Okay
16–19 Fair

DISCUSSION

1. What are some reasons you may fail to perceive, or perceive incorrectly, your commonplace world?
2. How much of our perception comes from experiences stored in our subconscious (those items at which you guessed)?
3. Is it important to perceive our immediate environment/surroundings accurately? Objectively? Why? Why not?

PURPOSE

To help you understand that recent events in your life affect the way you perceive the world.

PROCEDURE

1. In the space below, write about an event within a recent time period that has affected the way you perceive the present and, thus, your intra/interpersonal communication with For example, it might be a new job, a change of schools, a birth or death, a relationship, experience, accomplishment, decision, etc. Be very specific in your description.

2. Describe the ways this event has affected your perception, your communication, your opinion about yourself, and your values.
3. In what ways has this event caused you to alter your behavior? Explain.
4. Form small groups and discuss what each has written. Also discuss the following questions.

DISCUSSION

1. How does the way you see the world affect your communication on both the intrapersonal and interpersonal levels?
2. How can you relate this knowledge and insight to your personal, professional, and social lives?
3. Are you likely to let this event have a lasting effect, or will you soon forget it?

Perception Scavenger Hunt

PURPOSE

To encourage you to experience and utilize your senses.

PROCEDURE

Follow each of the instructions, using the senses indicated.

1. List the eye color of 3 people in this class.

    A. (Name)

    B. (Name)

    C. (Name)

2. List the shoe color of 3 people in this class.

    A. (Name)

    B. (Name)

    C. (Name)

3. Describe the feel of the hands of 2 of your friends (one male and one female). Describe both back and palms.

    A. (Name)

    B. (Name)

4. Describe the textures (feel) of 3 different types of clothing materials that you own.

    A.

    B.

    C.

5. Taste 2 foods you have not tasted before; name them and describe their taste.

    A.

    B.

6. Sit in the library, close your eyes, and count to 30. Then—with your eyes still closed—listen. Describe what you heard.

7. While still in the library, describe what you smell (keep your eyes closed while smelling).

8. Describe the fragrance of the cologne or perfume worn by 2 people you know.

   A.

   B.

9. Stand or sit outside where you live, with your eyes closed. Listen for 5–10 minutes. Describe the different things you hear.

10. Go to a supermarket.

    A. Walk through the produce section and list 5 things you smell.
    1.

    2.

    3.

    4.

    5.

    B. Walk down the cereal aisle—list the different smells.

11. Have someone at home give you 3 different spices to smell with your eyes closed. Try to identify the spices.

A.

B.

C.

Please answer the following:

1. What did you discover about your senses and the attention you pay to any or all of them?

2. Did you have any new discoveries? If so, what?

3. What did you learn from this activity that can help you better perceive the world around you?

What Hemisphere Are You In?

PURPOSE

To permit you to determine your dominant brain hemisphere.

PROCEDURE

For each of the following statements, indicate your *usual* preference.

YES or NO

_____ 1. When I read a newspaper article I like to read it from the beginning to the end.

_____ 2. When I read a newspaper article I like to skim through it and look at the photographs.

_____ 3. In most situations I am more logical and rational than I am aware of my feelings.

_____ 4. In most situations I am more aware of my feelings than I am logical and rational.

_____ 5. I am comfortable with numbers and symbols.

_____ 6. I have a weak sense of time.

YES or NO

_____	7.	I more easily see the differences between people, things, etc. than I can see the similarities.
_____	8.	I more easily see the similarities between people, things, etc. than I can see the differences.
_____	9.	I like to have a task "spelled out" in detail before I do it.
_____	10.	I like to know the overall purpose of a task before I do it.
_____	11.	I like to do work by myself.
_____	12.	I like to do work in groups.
_____	13.	I tend to see the logical progression when exploring a situation.
_____	14.	I tend to see the "overall picture" when exploring a situation.

Add up the total number of "Yes" answers for odd numbered (left hemisphere dominant) items: _____

Add up the total number of "Yes" answers for even numbered (right hemisphere dominant) items: _____

Higher number of "yes" items indicates your dominant hemisphere where the difference between the two scores is 3 or more.

DISCUSSION

1. Compare your results with others.
2. How does the culture encourage left hemisphere dominance?
3. What possible advantage would it be to be a more "integrated thinker" (both hemispheres closer to equally dominant)?
4. How can you go about developing your less dominant hemisphere?

Count the Squares

PURPOSE

To compare your perception with the perception of others, and to see how others can teach you to perceive.

PROCEDURE

1. Count the number of squares in the diagram below. How many squares are there?
2. Join a group, recount the squares and enter the total number of squares you see.

DISCUSSION

How does communicating with others affect our perception?

Improving Our Perceptual Awareness

In order to objectify our perceptions of the real world so that they are in alignment with what really is rather than the way we perceive them to be, we have to be aware. Such awareness is not easy. Constant awareness is probably impossible. Jon Kabat-Zinn, in his book *Wherever You Go There You Are*, writes about being "mindful" in our daily activities.

You might begin your journey toward awareness by taking some small steps. Set aside a brief time each day in which you plan to observe what is going on without having any expectations or making any judgments about what occurs. Gradually increase the number of times each day that you do this. You might then extend this process to an interaction that you plan with another individual. After you have spent some time on this technique, you might ask others to share their perceptions with you of some things that you have both observed. Stay open to just listening to what they have to say. From such a simple start, you will soon find yourself being more objective, and more open to what is really happening in the world.

Perception Checking

One specific approach to be more objective that we can begin today is described in the following activity. It is an approach to check out the difference between what another person means by a specific behavior and the meaning that we attach to it. This activity is one that you can do anytime you are confused by another person's words or behavior.

First step: Describe the behavior to the other person in objective, neutral language.

Second step: Indicate two possible explanations that you have made about the behavior.

Third step: Ask the person to tell you which explanation is correct.

Example: The situation might look like this:

Your friend said that she would meet you in front of the library at 9:00 A.M. today to study for the exam that you will both take tomorrow. But she failed to show. At 3:00 P.M. you ran into her in the cafeteria and she acted like you never had an appointment.

First step: (Describe the event objectively) "Hi Karen, we had planned yesterday in Bio to meet today in front of the library at 9:00 A.M. I was there from 8:55 until 9:10, but you never showed up."

Second step: (Offer two possible explanations of her behavior) "Either you misunderstood our plans or you had something else come up."

Third step: (Ask which explanation is correct) "Which was it?"

Such perception checking does not reverse the failed 9:00 A.M. appointment but it lets your friend know what you are thinking, and it allows her to explain her behavior. This takes the guessing out of her motives and allows you to communicate accurately about what occurred.

The Way We See Me

PURPOSE

To compare the way you see yourself with the way others see you.

PROCEDURE

1. Give copies of the questionnaire on the next pages to some of your relatives or friends.
2. Answer "The Way We See Me Questionnaire" as the items apply to you.
3. Take time to compare your questionnaire with each person who answered one.

DISCUSSION

1. What similarities did you notice among all questionnaire responses? Why?
2. What differences did you notice among all questionnaire responses? Why?
3. What did you learn about yourself from this activity?
4. What effect do our various perceptions of one another have on interpersonal communication?

THE WAY WE SEE ME QUESTIONNAIRE (SELF)

As part of a class assignment, I am distributing this questionnaire to some of my relatives and friends. It is designed to give me your impressions of my personality. I am attempting to compare the way other people see me with the way I see myself. While it may be difficult for you to express your impressions exactly, I would appreciate as frank a rating as you can give me.

This questionnaire should not take long to complete. First, try to construct an overall view of your impressions about my personality before answering the specific questions. Consider each item briefly and indicate the first choice that occurs to you. If you come to an item that you feel unable to answer with certainty, place a question mark, instead of a check, in one of the spaces to indicate a guess. However, please do answer every question. If you have comments that will help explain any of your answers, please use the space provided or write in the margins. Explanatory comments will be appreciated.

Please begin by considering my main strengths and weaknesses. Describe each as carefully as you can in the spaces below:

Main Strengths:

Main Weaknesses:

How well do the following words apply to me? Please checkmark the word/phrase that applies.

	Not at all	Slightly	Moderately	Rather well	Extremely well
Self-confident					
Tactful					
Irritable					
Quiet					
Emotionally variable					
Serious					
Energetic					
Well-adjusted					
Cooperative					
Prejudiced					
Unpredictable					

	Not at all	Slightly	Moderately	Rather well	Extremely well
Selfish					
Leader					
Considerate of others					
Tense					
Accepts criticism					
Aggressive					
Easy to get to know					
Imaginative					
Sense of humor					
Friendly					
Dogmatic					
Responsible					
Ambitious					
Physically attractive					
Sexually attractive					
Mature					
Trusting of others					
Open					

How accurately do these answers reflect your impressions of me?

How well do you feel you know me?

Additional Comments:

Respondent: ❐ Self
               ❐ Relative
               ❐ Friend

THE WAY WE SEE ME QUESTIONNAIRE
(RELATIVE OR FRIEND)

As part of a class assignment, I am distributing this questionnaire to some of my relatives and friends. It is designed to give me your impressions of my personality. I am attempting to compare the way other people see me with the way I see myself. While it may be difficult for you to express your impressions exactly, I would appreciate as frank a rating as you can give me.

This questionnaire should not take long to complete. First, try to construct an overall view of your impressions about my personality before answering the specific questions. Consider each item briefly and indicate the first choice that occurs to you. If you come to an item that you feel unable to answer with certainty, place a question mark, instead of a check, in one of the spaces to indicate a guess. However, please do answer every question. If you have comments that will help explain any of your answers, please use the space provided or write in the margins. Explanatory comments will be appreciated.

Please begin by considering my main strengths and weaknesses. Describe each as carefully as you can in the spaces below:

Main Strengths:

Main Weaknesses:

How well do the following words apply to me? Please checkmark the word/phrase that applies.

	Not at all	Slightly	Moderately	Rather well	Extremely well
Self-confident					
Tactful					
Irritable					
Quiet					
Emotionally variable					
Serious					
Energetic					
Well-adjusted					
Cooperative					
Prejudiced					
Unpredictable					

	Not at all	Slightly	Moderately	Rather well	Extremely well
Selfish					
Leader					
Considerate of others					
Tense					
Accepts criticism					
Aggressive					
Easy to get to know					
Imaginative					
Sense of humor					
Friendly					
Dogmatic					
Responsible					
Ambitious					
Physically attractive					
Sexually attractive					
Mature					
Trusting of others					
Open					

How accurately do these answers reflect your impressions of me?

How well do you feel you know me?

Additional Comments:

Respondent:　　❐　Self
　　　　　　　　❐　Relative
　　　　　　　　❐　Friend

THE WAY WE SEE ME QUESTIONNAIRE
(RELATIVE OR FRIEND)

As part of a class assignment, I am distributing this questionnaire to some of my relatives and friends. It is designed to give me your impressions of my personality. I am attempting to compare the way other people see me with the way I see myself. While it may be difficult for you to express your impressions exactly, I would appreciate as frank a rating as you can give me.

This questionnaire should not take long to complete. First, try to construct an overall view of your impressions about my personality before answering the specific questions. Consider each item briefly and indicate the first choice that occurs to you. If you come to an item that you feel unable to answer with certainty, place a question mark, instead of a check, in one of the spaces to indicate a guess. However, please do answer every question. If you have comments that will help explain any of your answers, please use the space provided or write in the margins. Explanatory comments will be appreciated.

Please begin by considering my main strengths and weaknesses. Describe each as carefully as you can in the spaces below:

Main Strengths:

Main Weaknesses:

How well do the following words apply to me? Please checkmark the word/phrase that applies.

	Not at all	Slightly	Moderately	Rather well	Extremely well
Self-confident					
Tactful					
Irritable					
Quiet					
Emotionally variable					
Serious					
Energetic					
Well-adjusted					
Cooperative					
Prejudiced					
Unpredictable					

	Not at all	Slightly	Moderately	Rather well	Extremely well
Selfish					
Leader					
Considerate of others					
Tense					
Accepts criticism					
Aggressive					
Easy to get to know					
Imaginative					
Sense of humor					
Friendly					
Dogmatic					
Responsible					
Ambitious					
Physically attractive					
Sexually attractive					
Mature					
Trusting of others					
Open					

How accurately do these answers reflect your impressions of me?

How well do you feel you know me?

Additional Comments:

Respondent: ❏ Self
             ❏ Relative
             ❏ Friend

The Whole Truth

PURPOSE

In this exercise, you are to examine your emotional responses to the following situations. How well are you able to project yourself into these situations and describe how you would actually respond? There is a tendency for us to be logical and describe how we would like to act, or how nobly we are supposed to act, but the test is to determine if we can accurately and honestly describe our first feelings—our emotional reactions to these situations.

PROCEDURE

Read about each situation and briefly describe your first reaction to each one in the space provided.

1. You are in a hurry. You drive to a school supply store to pick up some items for a quiz. You look for a parking place close to the store. The lot is full. But there are two parking places directly in front of the store that are occupied by just one car. The driver has left the car at an angle with part of it in both places. The parking stalls are clearly marked. There is no reason the car could not be parked so that another driver could use the valuable parking space.

   Was the driver being considerate of others? What are your feelings when you see something like this? What is your attitude toward the driver?

2. You are terribly busy at work. You stop long enough to dash across the street to pick up something at the store. You stand at the counter waiting. Behind the counter is a young girl reading a book. She apparently ignores you. You stand there for several minutes before you finally go to another checkout stand.

   What are your reactions and your feelings? What is your attitude toward the girl?

3. You are walking through a run-down section of a city. Lying against the wall of a building is a man with messed-up clothing and an empty wine bottle beside him. He is mumbling to himself.

What are your feelings? What is your attitude toward him?

DISCUSSION

In small groups, compare your reactions with others and determine what caused each of you to react as you did.

What disturbs men's minds is not events but their judgments on events. —*Epictetus*

PURPOSE

Now that you have had an opportunity to express your feelings about each of these situations, let's go a step further and see how the stories ended. These are based on true instances so they aren't as unusual as they might sound. Your task is to see how your feelings change once you gain a different perspective.

PROCEDURE

After reading the additional information about each situation below, write how your feelings or attitudes have changed.

1. You finally park your car. You are about to enter the store and see the driver of the car parked in two places run out, jump in the car, and drive away. Inside the store, the clerk tells you that there has just been a bad accident a mile away. The driver of the car who parked carelessly taking up two spaces had driven to the store to telephone the ambulance and the police. In his rush to get to a phone, he was not aware of the way he had parked.

    Any change in feeling now? How about your attitude toward the driver?

2. As you prepare to leave the store, the owner approaches the girl who had ignored you. After speaking a few words to her in French, he introduces her to the clerk who checked you out as a foreign student who will be living with his family during the next school year. The student was just waiting for a ride to the owner's home.

    Any change in feeling now? How about your attitude toward the girl?

3. A police ambulance pulls up. You learn that the man, a banker, was just hit on the head with the wine bottle and robbed.

Describe your feelings now. Any changes in attitude?

DISCUSSION

Return to your small groups and discuss how your attitudes or feelings changed after learning the additional facts.

Increasing Perceptual Understanding

PURPOSE

To allow the students an opportunity to practice perception checking.

PROCEDURE

1. Divide into small groups
2. Have each group member describe a situation when he/she was not clear about the meaning of another person's behavior.
3. Have each group member now offer a 3-step perception-checking response to each situation.

DISCUSSION

1. How does the first step of the process take the threat out of talking to the other person?
2. How does offering two possible explanations allow the other person to understand your perceptions?
3. How does asking a question at the end clarify what you want from the other?

Name _____

Date _____

Your professor may require this exercise to be handed in.

REACTIONS TO CHAPTER 3

1. List at least five reasons you perceive differently from everyone else.

2. Why do we study perception in a Communication class?

3. How will your new knowledge of perception help you to be a better communicator? Give an example using a specific person from your job, family, friends, or other relationships.

4. What are at least four things we can do to increase fidelity when we find that the persons with whom we are communicating have perceptions different from our own?

5. Indicate a recent event in which you might have used the perception-checking technique. How might the results have been different?

Nonverbal Communication

Nonverbal communication consists of relaying message units to augment, contradict, or replace verbal communication.

◈ Nonverbal Communication

General Definitions:

Relays messages from individual to individual or from object to individual.

> ***Example:*** Husband smiles at his wife.
> Red light signals vehicles to stop.

Can augment verbal communication.

> ***Example:*** A mother can shout at her child and simultaneously stamp her foot. Both her vocal utterance and physical gesture convey similar meanings.

Can contradict verbal communication.

> ***Example:*** A man can tell a woman that he loves her while unconsciously he is backing away from her.

Can replace verbal communication.

> ***Example:*** Visitors in foreign countries have often asked for and received directions through gesture.

THE IMPORTANCE OF NONVERBAL COMMUNICATION

Most of us already know a great deal about nonverbal communication. After all, we've been doing it since the instant we were born. We already know (or think we do) when someone's verbal message is contradicted by the nonverbal signals. And we almost always subconsciously choose the nonverbal message over the verbal!

Depending on which set of definitions we use, from 75 to 95 percent of all the communication that we do is nonverbal. With these two facts in mind (we already know much about nonverbal communication and we do an enormous amount of it), let's ask one more question: How good are we at communicating nonverbally?

If we are honest with ourselves, we may have to admit that we are not very effective at it. Many of our misunderstandings and our communication failures result from the errors we make in "reading" nonverbal communication.

And that is what this chapter is all about. Taking the knowledge you already have, let's learn how to make our own nonverbal communication more effective, and how to do a better job of interpreting the nonverbal language of others.

BARRIERS TO NONVERBAL COMMUNICATION

Because nonverbal communication is so important, you would think that people would be more aware of how to make effective use of it in their conversations, but they don't. Why don't they? We think that at least three barriers get in the way:

- A lack of awareness of our own nonverbal messages

- A lack of knowledge and training about nonverbal communication

- A tendency to assume that we understand each other's nonverbal communication

Lack of Awareness

A lack of awareness of our own nonverbal messages. Most of us tend to be unaware that we are always communicating nonverbally with everyone who can see or hear us. As soon as other persons notice us, they attach some meaning to what they see or hear. If they like what they hear or see, they attach positive value to us. If we seem similar to someone they like, they think well of us. The opposite can also occur if they don't like what they see. Much of our talking is an attempt to make sure that others see us as we want them to, not as they do.

In addition to the passive messages that we send to others, we also actively send messages to others about how we feel about them, every time that we communicate with them. For example, when I tell the person behind the ice cream counter that I want a vanilla ice cream cone, my nonverbal message will let the person know how I feel about her. Are we equal as people or is she my servant for the moment?

We may spend a lot of time carefully planning the words that we are going to say but our nonverbal messages may totally invalidate everything that we had intended.

Lack of Knowledge and Training

A lack of knowledge and training about nonverbal communication. The elocutionists of the 18th and 19th centuries were very much aware of the impact that their gestures, posture, and use of their voices had on audiences, and they received careful training to perfect those skills. With the more conversational style of modern speakers, we left behind the grand style of earlier speakers and we also forgot the understanding on which it was all built. Recently, communication experts have popularized nonverbal communication as a way of learning about others' behavior. Few, however, have indicated the need to be aware of and to understand our own nonverbal actions.

Although many courses are available for teaching how to speak, and a few courses and seminars are designed to help people to listen better, there is still little opportunity to learn how to use nonverbal communication more effectively.

Our Tendency to Assume

A tendency to assume that we understand each other's nonverbal communication. If you have already read about verbal communication (sending audio messages), you should be able to see the similar pattern with nonverbal communication. When others send messages, whether they are sent verbally or nonverbally, our tendency is to respond to them from our frame of reference. That means that we guess what they are saying and respond based on our guesses. For example, if we guess correctly that our friend's crossed arms mean that she is upset, we would respond correctly by quietly talking about what is bothering her. However, those symbols of crossed arms may merely mean that she is cold.

It is difficult not to see others as we see ourselves. Yet to be effective communicators, we need to know that we are all very different from each other, and that the purpose of communication is to discover our differences and similarities.

I learn a great deal by merely observing you, and letting you talk as long as you please, and taking note of what you do not say. —*T. S. Eliot*

YOU DON'T SAY

You arrive at work and a message awaits you at your desk. The boss wants to see you. You enter the grey walled office of your boss. He stands, arms folded, behind a large rectangular desk. He motions you to sit. He peers at you with a direct, unwavering stare.

The term "nonverbal" is commonly used to describe human and animal communication excepting those of spoken or written words. Our "nonverbal" communication, which is our manner of speaking without words, is partly taught, partly imitative, and partly instinctive. These "nonverbal" messages may repeat, contradict, complement, accent, or regulate that which we actually "say."

Let us look at the fact situation above. What would be your reaction? "Why is he staring at me?" "His arms are folded; why is he angry?" The direct stare is seen by many in this culture as a form of threat. However, while not unique, this is characteristic of our culture specifically. Staring, in addition, is considered a threat in many species of animals. Now, let us change slightly the fact situation above. Now, your boss stares, but also smiles and nods suggestively. What does he mean now? He may be expressing emotion, a possible raise, even sexual interest by the same stare when coupled by other nonverbal messages.

Nonverbal communication is quite possibly the most important part of the communicative process, for researchers now know that our actual words carry far less meaning than nonverbal cues. For example, repeat many times the following sentence, emphasizing different words in the sentence each time you do so: "I beat my spouse last night." Does not the meaning of the sentence change? The words themselves carry many meanings, depending upon nonverbal cues, in the case, inflection. Essentially, the study of nonverbal communication is broken down to:

- environmental clues
- spatial study
- physical appearance
- behavioral cues
- vocal qualities
- body motion or kinesics

Oculesics—Eye Contact and Facial Expression

A great deal is conveyed through our eyes and facial expression. However, we cannot isolate this study without considering all other bodily and environment cues. Facial expression is probably the most communicative of our body. Researchers have only recently discovered that the facial expressions made are extremely rapid and may not be consciously noticed in normal communication. They are, however, picked up by our subconscious faculties in giving meaning to the words used. By careful study, one can learn to notice expressions.

Of all facial cues, eye contact has found the most interest by researchers. Years of study have gone into characterizing and identifying pupil dilation. We know, for instance, that continued eye contact may signal arousal, interest, or attentiveness.

However, we do not as yet know the full extent of cultural aspects of such eye contact. For example, in our culture when we feel physically uncomfortable due to the proximity of others, we lower our eyes (traditionally though not always). We feel awkward or somehow invaded if someone stares intently at us. It is deemed a threat. Eye contact may differ from age to age and between sexes. Researchers are, however, not sure to what degree. It remains an open field for research and investigation.

The Environment

There is little doubt that the environment in which one speaks may contribute to the overall communicative process. Ponder for a moment how the size of the room, furniture arrangements, temperature, lighting, color of the walls, and even the space between persons may affect our desire to communicate or the openness of the communication.

High in the study of environmental clues is the study of **proxemics** or the investigation of how space between individuals may affect the communicative process between them. It appears that we culturally and instinctively maintain a protective perimeter of space between us and the outside world. While this space may differ from culture to culture, it may have its base in the protective instincts of our animalistic past. Researchers have isolated several distances and attached to them levels of communication. Between 0 and 18 inches, we traditionally allow our most intimate friends. We communicate on a "personal" level with those persons within 18 inches to 4 feet. This personal level is usually reserved to classmates or other persons at a party or meeting. A "social" distance is considered somewhere between 4 feet and 12 feet, this level being reserved to guests in living rooms, and so on. Finally, there appears an "impersonal" distance beyond 12 feet out to the limit of hearing, which does not seem to generate personal communication. These distances are not hard and fast but seem to differ with cultural, even physical, differences between individuals. When we are given the opportunity, we will naturally establish the distance appropriate with the topic of discussion and the nature of the relationship we have with the other person.

Kinesics—Behavior and Gestures

When we speak of gestures and body language, we deal with the heart of the study of nonverbal behavior. As in all nonverbal study, we note that such behavior is contextual and must not be isolated from the study of other "cues." We also note that the field of body language or kinesics is still ripe for eager and youthful research. For the most part, body language seems to reinforce facial communication. For instance, while our face may indicate what emotions we feel, the body gestures may indicate the intensity of that emotion. Think of the small child who frowns and stamps her foot. This body gesture study and body language itself seems to parallel elementary spoken language without the complexity of grammar, punctuation, or the like. Consider the way other individuals and ourselves stand. Do we point our body, so to speak, toward the source of a verbal message, or do we seem to lean away from the source? Do we cross both our arms and legs when faced with unwelcome vocality? What message is portrayed by an individual who slouches in his chair? Generally, he appears to lack interest in the conversation. He may, in fact, be intensely interested but his body language contradicts his motivation. Those communicating with him perceive this lack of interest and adjust accordingly, many times negatively, to the communicative process. However, what message is portrayed by an individual who leans forward, nodding occasionally?

When we speak of gestures, we usually speak of hand gestures, although other body parts may, in fact, gesture equally as well. In fact, some hand gestures may be used instead of words, such as the language of the deaf. Hand gestures may also indicate the intensity of the emotion felt.

Physcial Appearance and Dress

Here, as in most of the nonverbal communication studies, while researchers are aware of the power of physical appearance and dress on communication, they are yet unsure of the full role it plays. We know, for example, that appearance plays a part in the process as it influences responses to vocal messages. Appearance can be the determinative feature of our message, and may signal messages to others as to our own personality. To deny this importance is to deny the millions of dollars spent each year on perfumes, creams, oils, hair ornaments, contact lenses, beards, eye shadow, suits, clothes, toothpaste, mouthwash, and deodorant. These physical messages we give are many times called "Thing Communication" or "Object Language." Our clothing often determines the credibility of our message, as does our physical make-up. If we are going to speak to a business group, we dress conservatively and less comfortably to show confidence and personality. For example, how do we perceive the personality or individual who is dressed in a military uniform? How is that military person perceived differently from the judge in a black robe? Consider the length of someone's hair, or whether the beard or hair is unkempt or neatly trimmed.

Vocalics (Vocal Cues)

The last nonverbal cue to be discussed here, while certainly not the end of the study of nonverbal messages, is the area of vocal cues, or paralanguage. These vocal cues play a major role in assisting the listener in determining meaning. A vocal cue can be defined as an audible stimulus to a message that, while not using actual words, conveys a type of meaning. For example, consider the nervous man who speaks too fast or the angry person who begins speaking louder and louder. As we discussed before, the simple inflection in a sentence can greatly change the meaning of the message.

Nonverbal Communication

This most important aspect of message delivery is still wide open for scrutiny and research. Investigators have only reached the surface of a vastly interesting and meaningful study.

Nonverbal Cafeteria Exercise

PURPOSE

To demonstrate that nonverbal communication sends "clues, not facts."

PROCEDURE

1. With the following worksheet, select an interesting looking individual (whom you do not know) to observe. Try to pick someone who does not seem ready to move on, and station yourself far enough away so that you can *see* your subject but *not hear* what she is saying.
2. Observe the individual for as long as possible, remembering to be discreet, and record your impressions.
3. When the person looks as though she is getting ready to leave, approach her with a smile, confess your "spying," and check your observations. You'll be surprised how friendly a stranger can be when she discovers she's helping you with classwork.
4. When you return to class, compare your observations with your classmates.

NONVERBAL CAFETERIA OBSERVATION FORM

Basic Description	Appearance	Actual
Gender		
Age		
Major		
Bilingual		
Live with parents		
Political Party		
Sports		
Activities		
Veteran of military service		
Children		
Brothers, sisters		
Relationship to others at table		
Mood		
From out of state		
Type of car		
Name		
Type of employment		

PURPOSE

To determine what your personal space is, and to explore your feelings about your personal space when it is invaded.

PROCEDURE

1. With your partners, perform the following exercise. As you perform the exercise, examine your "feelings' or emotional responses.
2. Have a person of the same sex approach you from each of the given directions. Stop the partner when the distance between you is comfortable. Measure the approximate distance.

    a. Directly from the front.
    b. Directly from the left.
    c. Directly from the right.
    d. From a 45-degree angle from the left.
    e. From a 45-degree angle from the right.
    f. From the rear.

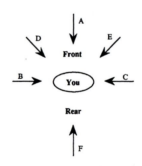

3. Repeat the same exercises with a person of the opposite sex.
4. From the front position allow the person to come too close. At this distance, engage the person in a conversation for at least one minute.
5. Again, take time to examine your feelings or emotional responses.

DISCUSSION

1. What differences in your body space and in your emotional responses did direction make?
2. What difference did the sex of your partner make?
3. What other factors could influence the size of your "body bubble"?
4. How did you feel when your personal space was invaded?
5. How did you and your partner react when your space was invaded?
6. How can differences in the size of personal space affect communication between people and cultures?

Eye Contact and Body Position Activity

PURPOSE

To determine feelings associated with too much and too little eye contact, to find what is "normal" eye contact and to examine feelings associated with "talking down" versus "talking up."

PROCEDURE

1. Select a partner and carry on a discussion for about one minute in each of the following positions; note your feelings associated with each.

    a.   side by side with *no eye contact*
    b.   face to face with *no eye contact*
    c.   face to face with *constant eye contact*
    d.   one standing and one sitting facing each other with "normal eye contact."
    e.   reverse the standing and sitting positions again with "normal eye contact."

DISCUSSION

1.   Which did you find more difficult: no eye contact or constant eye contact? Why?
2.   Which felt more uncomfortable: talking "down" or talking "up?" Why?
3.   In what kinds of situations might you find yourself talking "down" or "up," and what can you do about it?
4.   What is "normal" eye contact? When do you look at the other person and when do you look away?

PURPOSE

To compare and contrast nonverbal behaviors and expectations in a variety of social settings.

PROCEDURE

Read the following scenario below and then list the appropriate nonverbal behavior as understood by *your own cultural background*.

Scenario: You are about to have a foreign exchange student stay with you: they have asked you for some guidelines regarding the following situations. Remember, provide direction as *you* understand what is appropriate from *your cultural background*. Write down all acceptable variations.

1.   Greetings/introductions:

   a.   boss

   b.   senior citizen

   c.   "new person" at a party

   d.   stranger in a public place

2.   Saying goodbye to your partner/spouse in a public place:

3. Clothing for:

    a. school

    b. religious ceremony

    c. dinner at a good friend's house

4. Dressing for a funeral:

    a. women

    b. men

5. Seating:

    a. a group of men at the movies

    b. a group of women at the movies

DISCUSSION

Form groups of 4–6 and compare and contrast your answers.

1. What was similar? What was different?
2. Were there differences based on gender?
3. What might these nonverbal expectations say about cultural values such as formality, informality, modesty, status, etc?
4. Were there any generational differences?

Breaking Nonverbal Rules

PURPOSE

To become better acquainted with some of the rules of nonverbal communication, and to analyze the effects of breaking such rules.

PROCEDURE

Read the following rules and decide which you want to break. Break the rule(s) with people that you do not know, and be aware of their responses. Record their responses and your feelings.

The rules:

1. Upon entering an elevator, turn towards the door and stare at it. Do not talk or make contact with the others in the elevator.
2. When sitting down in a cafeteria, take a seat that is as far away from the next person as possible.
3. When sitting next to someone, do not invade their private space with your body or belongings.
4. When sitting directly across from people, do not stare at them for more than a second or two.
5. Members of the opposite sex should not stare at the various sexual parts of the other person's body while that person is watching you.
6. When strangers are talking, do not enter their group.
7. Keep the appropriate distance when talking to someone: closer for intimate topics, but never so close that you invade the other person's space.
8. When talking in an occupied area, lower your voice so that you do not disturb others with your conversation.
9. When talking to someone, do not stare at their eyes/face. Also don't avoid their glance completely.
10. When talking to someone, do not touch them more than absolutely necessary.

These are only some of the nonverbal rules in our culture. If you choose to break one on the list, please check with your instructor before doing the project.

NOTE: Do not break any rules that would infringe on the rights of others, or **that would put you in any type** of danger.

DISCUSSION

1. What were the reactions of others to your breaking the rules?
2. What were your feelings when you broke the rules?
3. How can not knowing the rules of a particular situation or culture affect communication?

Approachable/Non-Approachable Nonverbal Communication

PURPOSE

To give you a chance to explore what nonverbal communication you and others may send which communicates you or they may be "approachable" and "non-approachable."

PROCEDURE

1. Form a small group and brainstorm all of the nonverbal cues that you might receive from someone else that would communicate to you that the person is "non-approachable." Be sure to consider all of the following categories of nonverbal communication:

   a. Haptics—touch
   b. Oculesics—facial expression and eye contact
   c. Kinesics—movement
   d. Proxemics—space, including personal space
   e. Vocalics—vocal factors (paralanguage)
   f. Posture
   g. Chronemics (use of time)
   h. Object language (including clothing, jewelry, furniture, etc.)
   i. Environment

2. Now have your group brainstorm all of the nonverbal cues that you might perceive from someone else that would communicate to you that the person is "approachable." Again, be sure to consider all of the above categories.

3. Which of these "approachable" cues involves the least amount of risk for the sender?

DISCUSSION

1. How can appearing "approachable" help in establishing communication with people we don't know?

2. How many of the nonverbal "non-approachable" cues might you have been sending without ever knowing it?

3. How might "approachable" nonverbal cues help someone overcome their shyness?

Nonverbal Communication Activity
Can You Tell How I Feel?

PURPOSE

To demonstrate how we communicate our feelings nonverbally and to help you become more aware of the various ways we communicate nonverbally.

PROCEDURE

1. Arrange the class into inner and outer circles, with students facing each other.
2. Each student will be given a sheet of emotions, lettered from A to K.
3. The inner circle will begin each rotation by being the message sender, and will communicate *verbally* about some topic selected by the class or by the individual. While doing so, they should communicate the designated emotion using nonverbal means, (e.g., tone of voice, gestures, eye contact, facial expressions).
4. The persons in the outer circle will listen to the message being communicated, while at the same time communicating their emotion nonverbally to the sender.
5. They will then change roles and the outer circle will communicate a verbal message and also the designated nonverbal emotion to the inner circle.
6. The inner circle persons will listen to the message being communicated while at the same time communicating their emotion nonverbally to the sender.
7. Both people will then try to identify the emotion that was being communicated by their partner and confirm with their partner the emotion that they intended to communicate.
8. The outer circle will then rotate one person, and the new pairs will begin again with the next emotion indicated on their lists.

DISCUSSION

Divide into groups and have them discuss the following:

1. Which emotions were easier to communicate and to understand, both as sender and receiver, and how were they communicated?
2. Which emotions were harder to communicate and to understand, both as a sender and receiver, and how were they communicated?
3. Why is it important to be aware of these various ways we communicate our emotions nonverbally?
4. Are there any conclusions we can make about how males and females communicate emotions nonverbally?

REACTIONS TO CHAPTER 4

1. Why is an understanding of nonverbal communication absolutely essential to high fidelity communication?

2. Which generally tells the truth of a message—verbal or nonverbal communication? Why?

3. What might be some of the reasons that a nonverbal signal might have different meanings for people in different situations?

Using Language

5

As you have seen so far, our concern is to help you improve your interpersonal communication. This chapter shows the role that language plays in those encounters. Do you always understand what others are saying to you? Are you always understood by others? If you're like most of us, the answer to these two questions is an emphatic "No." When two people speak the same language, share the culture, and experience similar incidents in their lives, why is it that one person can walk away confident that she has clearly communicated and the other stand in bewilderment wondering what was just said? In order to understand the problems that arise from taking our language abilities for granted, it will be necessary for us to first define a few concepts.

◆ Language

An established and accepted set of symbols and structure used for the transfer of meaning. (English, Spanish, Navajo, Farsi)

◆ Denotation

The commonly accepted definition of a word, as in the dictionary definition. (House = Dwelling)

◆ Connotation

The feeling and emotions that we associate with a word. (House = "Home")

◆ Linguistics

The study of language.

◆ Semantics

The study of meaning.

◆ General Semantics

The field of study that says language influences behavior.

THE IMPORTANCE OF USING LANGUAGE EFFECTIVELY

Language Is Power

The study of how people have used language must certainly bring us to the conclusion that the "pen is mightier than the sword." Books, newspapers, and pamphlets have been so powerful that dictators waste no time banning and burning them and imprisoning those who seek freedom of the press.

What happens to you as you read, "The green, vile-looking pus oozed from the cut on the victim's arm"? How do you feel when someone calls you a dirty name? If you're like most of us, you can't help but react negatively and strongly.

We speak to be heard, to be listened to, to be understood. Our energies in sending symbols are spent in the presence of someone who can hear the results. We want something. Over 2,000 years ago the philosopher Aristotle said, "All speech is persuasive in nature." And so it is. We communicate to get our needs met. Whether that is strengthening a relationship, asking directions, or arguing with a friend, sending information through symbols to another is a way of persuading, thus we say that language is purposeful.

It is difficult to deny the power of language. In this chapter, we will examine how we can use language intrapersonally and interpersonally. Additionally, we will examine the extent to which language influences, and is influenced by, our culture.

Intrapersonal Use of Language

Think for a moment about the last vacation that you took, the party that you attended, or the success that you had. What came to your mind? Did you close your eyes and see the entire experience played back as if you had just begun your video cassette player? A few people may have answered yes to that question; for most of us, however, we probably began by saying to ourselves, "Let's see—that was when. . . ." Whether you then actually saw pictures or continued to recall the experience based on words, your thinking was either in part or wholly influenced by your manipulation of language.

Thinking is dependent, for most of us, on the use of language. The more successful we are in using language, the more successful we are going to be in thinking.

One of the important aspects of thinking that requires effective use of language is our ability to reason. Reasoning involves at least two steps: observation and inference. When we begin our reasoning process, we begin with an observation or with a statement (assumption) based on someone else's observation. These observations can also be called facts, and are subject to errors that we have already described in the chapter on perception.

The second step in reasoning is inferring. In this step, we use language to connect the observable fact to the unobservable conclusion. For example, you see your friend on April 15. You know that he went to see a tax advisor today. He looks sad and you hear him say that he doesn't know where he is going to come up with that much money. So far you have had a number of observable facts to deal with. You may infer that he has to pay more money for his income taxes. How did you come to that conclusion? You used language to relate the observable facts with outcomes related to each of those facts, until you narrowed the probable outcomes to your best guess.

Our ability to use language gives us more choice in the number of outcomes we can match with the facts that we observe. It also gives us a way of discounting or eliminating outcomes that are not appropriate. In other words, the power of reasoning depends on effective use of language.

Language Is Symbolic

While this may seem to be quite apparent, it is of astonishing importance. Words do not have any meaning in and of themselves. They are void of meaning. The symbols D-O-G are not the animal that barks and answers to the name "Rover." The letters (symbols) represent the animal only when our culture/society agrees that they represent the reality. There is no living, breathing thing in the symbols themselves. There is only the meaning that we attach to them. This is why we say, "Words don't mean; people mean." Indeed, if we simply reverse the symbols D-O-G, we must form an entirely new concept in our minds. But notice, it isn't the word that has meaning, it's us. Some of our exercises in this chapter will point out the dangers of forgetting this important lesson.

Language Is Learned

It is also important to realize that language is learned. Words, as symbols, must be learned in a context. While some are easily stored in our memory for future use (book, mother, day, food) many are so complex as to defy simply defining (is, to, be, the) and when you compound this with the idea that language (thus, words) is always changing (bad, cool, gay, hip), it's no wonder that we often misunderstand another's intended "meaning." To further complicate matters, we have to consider the importance of how we learned the word. If you had a pleasurable experience when you learned the word "cat" (soft, purring, cute), your image of "cat" will be forever influenced by that experience. However, if your experience was negative (scratches, biting, fleas, catbox), think how differently the symbol "cat" will affect you. Can a word that you assign meaning to affect you? For an answer to this question, your instructor will have you participate in an exercise designed to show the difference between **connotation** and **denotation**.

> I know you believe you understand
> what you think I said,
> but I'm not sure you realize that
> what you heard is not what I meant.

Perhaps there is a need to clarify general semantics. Too often we hear, "Oh, we're only arguing semantics." Or, "Let's not get hung up on semantics." The implication is that the problem is a small one, but matters of meaning can have far-reaching implications. Those of us who study language will be the first to tell you that words affect behavior. For instance, would you care to stop by my house for a slice of dead cow? Probably not, but most of you have enjoyed a barbecued steak. Do the words make a difference? You bet they do. This is no small matter, this "semantics." It can determine our entire perception of "reality" and that leads us to a definition that will not only help us to understand general semantics, but will set the stage for you to learn the importance of language in our daily communication. What I call something can cause you to perceive it differently. Semanticists carry this idea to the word to associate with it. Is it a thing without a name? This argument will be further developed in the chapter as you study the power of words.

BARRIERS TO USING LANGUAGE

Some people consider barriers to communication as roadblocks, that is, some obstacle that gets between what we intend to say and what is understood by the receiver. Language is much more complicated than the roadblock analogy. Many of the language barriers occur in our minds as we consider what we intend to say. These main barriers are described below.

Confusion Between Language and the Real World

If I write that I plan to scratch my finger nails along the chalk board and you immediately feel a cold shiver down your spine, it is because you confused what I said for the reality of my doing it. Now, such a reaction is not necessarily bad. As a matter of fact, if you were unable to react in such a manner, you probably would not enjoy reading a good book.

However, when we assume that the word we hear is exactly the same as the real-world counterpart that it describes, we are in trouble. To understand what we mean here, pretend that you are planning to hike up a mountain and you have a trail map in front of you. You note that there is a moderate elevation gain and a small stream that you will have to ford. You consider that these representations on the map are exactly the way it will be, and feel that you will have no difficulty on the hike. Once you set forth into the real world, however, you soon learn that the temperature is 92 degrees and the stream is 10 feet wide, five feet deep, and raging down the mountain. We very often make the same mistakes in the use of our language to describe the world around us.

An example of such confusion is found in the word "is." When you say, "He *is* a professional football player," what do you mean? To most people, the word "is" takes the place of "equals." Therefore, the meaning in the sentence is that "He equals professional football player." He is therefore not a father, brother, husband, student, or anything else at the moment. Additionally, he "equals" professional football player as *you* see it to mean, which may be different from professional football player as *I* see it to mean.

Our language should be considered as a description of the real world the way maps are a description of the real world. Maps only tell us a small part of what really exists. Our language has the same limitation.

Allness Attitude

Just as maps are incapable of telling everything that there is to tell about the territory, language is incapable of telling everything that there is to tell about the way you feel about someone, or how to do something that you have learned over many years of practice and effort. You can give us an idea through language of the broad boundaries. However, it is not possible for you to fill in every possible detail.

When people have an **allness attitude,** they act as though they have communicated everything that there is to say to another about a topic, and then they expect that the other person will have exactly the same reaction to that topic that they have. When the other person fails to see it as they do, they blame the other person rather than recognizing that the other person only got part of the picture.

Frozen Evaluation

When we think about something the way that it was and describe it now as though it had never changed, we are guilty of **frozen evaluation.** Because language describes things, ideas, and feelings, we often get hooked on the description and forget that everything in the real world constantly changes. So we run around with a lot of outdated descriptions in our heads that we haven't recently checked out with reality.

People who are constantly talking about the way things should be (as in the "good old days") are unwilling to give up the old descriptions and look at what is happening now. If you think of the boy who was the eighth-grade clown as the same person you knew six or ten years ago, you are going to have problems talking to someone about him who sees him as he is today.

Labeling

Labeling is where the sender of a message stereotypes someone and, rather than describe the behaviors, merely takes the easy path and says "Oh, he's a _____." When the receiver hears this label, he becomes the victim of the sender's laziness. Rather than let the receiver find out for himself what the other person is like, the sender, by labeling, has already placed in the receiver's mind the idea of the label. Let's take the label "jock" for an example. As soon as you hear, "That new kid in my class is a jock," you've begun to form an image. This prejudging is extremely dangerous because even before you've met the new student, you've probably created an image that could well be wrong. He must be big, athletic, in school only for sports, doesn't care about classes, and may not be too bright. What a terrible judgment to form based only on someone's care-

> For evil, then, as well as for good, words make us the human beings we actually are. Deprived of language, we should be dogs or monkeys. Possessing language, we are men and women able to persevere in crime no less than in heroic virtue, capable of intellectual achievements beyond the scope of any animal, but at the same time capable of systematic silliness and stupidity such as no dumb beast could ever dream of. —A. Huxley

less use of language. You know full well that all athletes are not big. Look at wrestlers in the lightweight division, or gymnasts or archers or golfers. You also know that all athletes are not in school just for sports. Many are involved in several extracurricular activities. Sports may be only one of several. You also know that many student athletes are outstanding scholars, earning excellent grades in even the most difficult classes. Many end up on the Dean's List for academic excellence, and many receive scholastic scholarships. Pat Hayden (ex-professional football player) was a Rhodes Scholar. And did we say "he"? How careless of us, because student athletes can, of course, be women. Do you see what can happen when labels are used? They are convenient, handy, and easy to use, but they are real road blocks to being an accurate communicator. In addition to labels, your instructor will show you the dangers inherent in confusing assumptions and judgments as "facts." Some of the activities that she may assign are the Semantics of Prejudice, the Hidden Assumptions Test, and the Uncritical Inference Test.

Polarization

This barrier occurs because of the nature of our language, English. Over the years English has evolved to a point where we have been forced to speak and think in extremes. The "middle ground" has been taken from us because we have few words to express the ideas that fall in the middle. Example: What word is the opposite of leader? Now, tell us what word is in-between? More difficult isn't it? Your instructor will have you participate in a brief activity called **polarization** to further explain this barrier.

Sexist Language Activity

PURPOSE

To explore the words used to describe both sexes that prompt both negative and positive reactions in the people described.

PROCEDURE

1. Divide into same-sex small groups.
2. Each group should brainstorm a list of words that they use to describe members of the opposite sex in a negative, demeaning way.
3. Each group should then list the demeaning words that they have heard the opposite sex use for them, and their reactions to these words.
4. Each group should then develop a list of words they would prefer to be called by the opposite sex.
5. As a full class, discuss each group's list and the feelings about the words listed.

DISCUSSION

1. How do the negative words make generalizations about the people they describe?
2. How do the negative words dehumanize the people they describe?
3. What are the differences between the negative and the preferred words?
4. How can the words we use to describe people influence their self-concept and their behavior?
5. How accurate do the words we use describe our perceptions?
6. What can we do to avoid sexist language when talking about our perceptions?

Language is the dress of thought. —*S. Johnson*

PURPOSE

To examine your own semantic reactions to terms and enable you to see how each of us experiences semantic noise.

PROCEDURE

Following a list of 22 terms. Beside each term, place a checkmark that corresponds to your immediate reaction to that word according to the scale indicated. Remember that the intent of the activity is to allow you to examine your semantic reactions, so be as honest in marking your reaction as you can. Your immediate reaction is usually the most reliable.

Reaction	Hightly Positive +2	Slightly Positive +1	Neutral or No Reaction 0	Slightly Negative −1	Highly Negative −2
1. patriotism					
2. breast					
3. pusillanimous					
4. love					
5. communism					
6. Caucasian					
7. Mexican					
8. bureaucracy					
9. speech					
10. friendship					
11. chauvinist					
12. hottie					
13. intercourse					
14. cancer					

	Hightly Positive	Slightly Positive	Neutral or No Reaction	Slightly Negative	Highly Negative
15. exacerbate					
16. gay					
17. cum laude					
18. seersucker					
19. Chicano					
20. skinhead					
21. white trash					
22. jock					
23.					
24.					

DISCUSSION

Now that you have completed the list, you will have a chance to compare your reactions with another member of the class and discuss the following questions:

1. How did you react to the various words?
2. Why did you react as you did? On what was your reaction based?
3. How can reaction to words (semantic reactions) affect communication?
4. With respect to semantic reactions, what suggestions could you make to improve communication?
5. What variables—i.e., sex, race, religion, income, age—influenced your responses?

Hidden Assumptions Test

PURPOSE

To discover fallacies of thinking based on hidden assumptions and overgeneralizations.

PROCEDURE

1. This is a timed test. Answer the questions as quickly as possible.
2. Once you have answered, go on to the next question. Do not go back to change any answer.

1. Each country has its own "Independence Day." Do they have a 4th of July in England? _____

2. How many birthdays does the average man have? _____

3. Can a man living in Winston-Salem, North Carolina be buried west of the Mississippi? _____

4. If you only had one match and entered a room in which there was a kerosene lamp, an oil heater, and a wood burning stove, which would you light first?

5. Some months have 30 days, some have 31. How many have 28?

6. If a doctor gave you three pills and told you to take one every half hour, how long would the pills last?

7. A house is built so that each side has a southern exposure. If a bear were to wander by the house, most likely the color of the bear would be _____.

8. How far can a dog run into the forest?

9. I have in my hand two U.S. coins which total 55 cents in value. One is not a nickel. What are the two coins?

10. A farmer has 17 sheep. All but nine died. How many does he have left?

11. Two men play chess. They played five games and each man won the same number of games. There were no ties. How can this be?

12. Take two apples from three apples and what do you get?

13. Divide 30 by one-half and add 10. What is the answer?

14. An archaeologist claimed she found gold coins dated 46 B.C. Do you think she did and why?

15. An airplane crashed exactly on the U.S.-Mexican border. Where would they bury the survivors?

16. How many animals of each species did Moses take aboard the ark with him?

17. Is it legal in California for a man to marry his widow's sister?

18. How much dirt may be removed from a hole that is 6 ft. deep, 2 ft. wide, and 10 ft. long?

19. If your bedroom were pitch dark and you needed a matching pair of socks, how many socks would you need to take out of the bureau drawer if there are 25 white and 25 blue?

20. If 3 cats kill 3 rats in 3 minutes, how long will it take 100 cats to kill 100 rats?

21. If it takes 10 men 10 days to dig a hole, how long will it take five men to dig half a hole?

22. Explain the following true boast: "In my bedroom, the nearest lamp that I usually keep turned on is 12 feet away from my bed. Alone in the room, without using any special devices, I can turn out the light on that lamp and get into bed before the room is dark."

23. A doctor refuses to operate on a patient who has been injured in an auto accident in which the patient's father was killed. The doctor refuses to operate because the patient is the doctor's son. How can this be?

24. There are 12 one-cent stamps in a dozen, but how many two-cent stamps are there in a dozen?

26. Which is correct: 7 and 8 are 13 or 7 and 8 is 13?

27. You have four nines (9, 9, 9, 9). Arrange them to total 100. You may use any of the arithmetical processes (addition, subtraction, multiplication, or division). Each nine must be used once.

DISCUSSION

1. Were you surprised at how many questions you could not answer?
2. Were you surprised at how many questions you answered correctly/incorrectly?
3. What did this test tell you about the assumptions you make?

William V. Haney

PURPOSE

To demonstrate the assumptions/inferences we make upon hearing or reading words.

PROCEDURE

This test is designed to determine your ability to think *accurately* and *carefully*. Since it is very probable that you have never taken this type of test before, failure to read the instructions **extremely carefully** may lower your score.

1. You will read a brief story. Assume that all of the information presented in the story is definitely *accurate* and *true*. Read the story carefully. You may refer back to the story whenever you wish.
2. You will then read statements about the story. Answer them in numerical order. **Do not go back** to fill in answers or to change answers. This will only distort your test score.
3. After you read each statement carefully, determine whether the statement is:
    a. "T"—meaning: on the basis of the *information presented in the story the statement is **definitely true***.
    b. "F"—meaning: On the basis of the *information presented in the story the statement is **definitely false***.
    c. "?"—meaning: The statement may be true (or false) but on the basis of the *information presented in the story* you cannot be *definitely certain*. (If any part of the statement is doubtful, mark the statement "?".)
4. Indicate your answer by circling either "T" or "F" or "?" opposite the statement.

STORY A

The only car parked in front of 619 Oak Street is a black one. The words "James M. Curley, M.D." are spelled in small gold letters across the left front door of that car.

Statements about the story

1.	The color of the car in front of 619 Oak Street is black.	T	F	?
2.	There is no lettering on the left front door of the car parked in front of 619 Oak Street.	T	F	?

Excerpted with permission from "The Uncritical Inference Test" by William V. Haney as it appears in William V. Haney, COMMUNICATION AND ORGANIZATIONAL BEHAVIOR, 3rd edition (Homewood, IL: Richard D. Irwin, Inc., 1973).

3. Someone is ill at 619 Oak Street.   T   F   ?
4. The black car parked in front of 619 Oak Street belongs to James M. Curley.   T   F   ?

Remember: Answer **only** on the basis of the information presented in the story. Refrain from answering as you think it **might** have happened. Answer each statement in numerical order. Do not go back to fill in or to change answers.

STORY B

A business man had just turned off the lights in the store when a man appeared and demanded money. The owner opened a cash register. The contents of the cash register were scooped up and the man sped away. A member of the police force was notified promptly.

Statements about Story B

1.	A man appeared after the owner had turned off his store lights.	T	F	?
2.	The robber was a *man*.	T	F	?
3.	The man who appeared did not demand money.	T	F	?
4.	The man who opened the cash register was the owner.	T	F	?
5.	Someone opened a cash register.	T	F	?
6.	After the man who demanded the money scooped up the contents of the cash register, he ran away.	T	F	?
7.	While the cash register contained money, the story does *not* state *how much*.	T	F	?
8.	The robber opened the cash register.	T	F	?
9.	After the store lights were turned off a man appeared.	T	F	?
10.	The robber did not take the money with him.	T	F	?
11.	The owner opened a cash register.	T	F	?
12.	The age of the store owner was not revealed in the story.	T	F	?
13.	The story concerns a series of events in which only three persons are referred to: the owner of the store, a man who demanded money, and a member of the police force.	T	F	?
14.	The following events were included in the story: someone demanded money, a cash register was opened, its contents were scooped up, and a man dashed out of the store.	T	F	?

DISCUSSION

1. Were you surprised at the number of assumptions and inferences you made?
2. Did certain types of words cause you to believe you understood their meaning?
3. What are the implications to your everyday language?

Excerpted with permission from "The Uncritical Inference Test" by William V. Haney as it appears in William V. Haney, COMMUNICATION AND ORGANIZATIONAL BEHAVIOR, 3rd edition (Homewood, IL: Richard D. Irwin, Inc., 1973).

Polarization

PURPOSE

To demonstrate that language forces us to speak and think in a polarized manner.

PROCEDURE

Fill in the opposites for the words below. Then try to find an in-between word for the opposites and write the words in the middle column.

WORD	IN-BETWEEN	OPPOSITE
tall		
heavy		
strong		
happy		
legal		
leader		
success		
wealthy		
woman		
beautiful		
black		
easy		
teacher		

DISCUSSION

1. Which is harder to find—an opposite word or an in-between word?
2. Which words are more descriptive—the polar opposites or the in-between words?
3. Is our language structured to make us think in polar opposites?

Owning My Communication

PURPOSE

To demonstrate that substituting the word "I" for the word "you" (changing the frame of reference) can improve communication.

PROCEDURE

Read the sentences below, which contain the word "you." Note the critical tone that the sentence assumes because of the use of the word "you."

Rewrite the sentences, substituting the word "I" and changing the phrase where necessary, and see if that neutralizes the tone of the sentence.

"YOU" Messages

1. You always give me another job to do before I finish the one I have.

2. You never pick up your clothes

3. You don't make an effort to get along with my friends.

4. You never show up on time.

5. Your tests are unreasonable.

6. You wasted your money on that.

7. You expect too much from me.

8. Why can't you communicate?

9. Why are you so angry?

10. You hurt my feelings.

"I" Messages

ex: *I need a break between projects.*

ex: *I am frustrated with the mess from these clothes.*

DISCUSSION

1. What makes changing the frame of reference difficult?
2. Why do we tend to use "you"?
3. Consider some recent situations where you could have changed the frame of reference. How would the outcome have changed?

The Slang Test

PURPOSE

To examine the way words mean different things to different people, and the way slang changes with time.

PROCEDURE

Circle the letter for what you think is the correct answer for each term.

1. This food is dank.
   a. awful
   b. good
   c. cold

2. Let's bounce.
   a. dance
   b. play basketball
   c. leave

3. It's tight.
   a. doesn't fit
   b. good
   c. bad

4. Gimme the 411.
   a. Give me the phone number.
   b. Let me know the information.
   c. Give me the phone.

5. Can I get your digits?
   a. measurements
   b. address
   c. phone number

6. What a Betty!
   a. a good cook
   b. good looking girl
   c. a bad gambling debt

7. He got game.
   a. He has the girls.
   b. He's good at sports.
   c. He lies.

8. That's off the chain.
   a. wild
   b. stupid
   c. cool

9. Why you trippin?
   a. Why are you stumbling?
   b. Why are you acting stupid?
   c. Why are you dressed that way?

10. That's burned out.
    a. ugly
    b. ridiculous
    c. over-cooked

11. Dang, you got years.
    a. intelligence
    b. experience
    c. nice clothes

12. Pimp my ride.
    a. Give me a ride.
    b. Fix up my car.
    c. Pick up my girlfriend and me.

13. You so fly.
    a. You're busy.
    b. You're a pest.
    c. looking good

14. Chicken head
    a. You like to eat chicken.
    b. ugly girl
    c. stuck-up girl

15. I give you props.
   a. money
   b. You need help.
   c. positive reaction

16. Let's cheese-it.
   a. eat
   b. get out of here
   c. rest

17. He's got a six-pack.
   a. gun
   b. well-developed abs
   c. beer

18. Throw up your set.
   a. Show your gang signs.
   b. Put up your fists.
   c. Bet your car.

19. Are you down?
   a. in a bad mood
   b. placed your bet
   c. in favor of it

20. He's a big timer.
   a. ex-con
   b. rich person under 30
   c. famous

21. That's pimp.
   a. nice or cool
   b. cheap
   c. sleazy

22. You're bling-blinging.
   a. not making sense
   b. talking too much
   c. wearing a lot of gold

23. Nice kicks.
   a. shoes
   b. moves
   c. dancer

24. What's the skuttlebut?
   a. drugs
   b. rumor
   c. food

25. Her idea was a real boondoggle.
   a. creative
   b. good
   c. poor

26. Let's boogie.
   a. have sex
   b. dance
   c. leave

27. She's a snazzy dresser.
   a. stylish
   b. sexy
   c. tasteless

28. He's a Jackson.
   a. criminal
   b. good dancer
   c. good looking

29. She's got ice.
   a. bad personality
   b. diamonds
   c. stuck up

DISCUSSION

1. Were you surprised at the number of questions you had to guess at?
2. What causes words to change meaning?
3. Why don't meanings stay the same?
4. How has slang changed over the years?

PURPOSE

To demonstrate the power of words and how people can use words to not only make themselves appear more intelligent, but to confuse an issue. This type of deliberately misleading language is something that any communicator who desires to be viewed as honest would certainly avoid.

PROCEDURE

This technical writing kit is based on the Simplified Integrated Modular Prose (SIMP) writing system. Using this kit, anyone who can count up to 10 can write as many as 40,000 discrete, well-balanced, grammatically correct sentences packed with EMBS terms and pedagogic gobbledygook.

To put SIMP to work, arrange the modules in A-B-C-D order. Make up four numbers, 7162 for example, and read Phrase 7 off Table A, Phrase 1 off Table B, etc. The result is a SIMP sentence. After you have mastered the basic technique you can realize the full potential of SIMP by arranging the modules in D-B-C-A order. In these advanced configurations some additional commas may be required.

SIMPLIFIED INTEGRATED MODULAR PROSE (SIMP)

SIMP Table A

1. A systematized basis upon which to evaluate competencies and outcomes

2. Initiation and maintenance of a comprehensive, flexible syllabus

3. A curricular formation of meaningful conceptual patterns

4. A ramification of commensurate behavioral objectives

5. A rational entailing subtopic analyses of psychomotor, cognitive, and affective domains

6. A noncimitant insight into undergirded knowledge transfer

7. The thrust of instructional objectives which preclude assumed

8. Any reasonably consistent doctrinal guide for curricular innovation

9. The identification of functional modes that equate with educational outcomes

10. A clarifying technique reformulated by the component group

SIMP Table B

1. According to EMBS procedures
2. Technically speaking
3. Based on integral exponential considerations
4. As a resultant implication
5. In respect to specific goals
6. In this regard
7. Relative to the needs assessment program
8. On the other hand
9. Definitively stated
10. In essence then

SIMP Table C

1. Must be based upon developmental conditions and standards with
2. Is further compounded by noncreative concept formulation for
3. Adds vertical organization in complex orientation interplay with
4. Presents extremely interesting subinterval controls to
5. Recognizes and enhances the maximization of individual potential for
6. Effects a significant implementation to functional performance criteria and
7. Necessitates correlative expertise in specialized areas of
8. Adds dimensional increments to the relevance of theory acquisition for
9. Predicates a viable analysis of multiphasic maturation studies to
10. Postulates that the degree of requisite content mastery is directly proportional to

SIMP Table D

1. The philosophy of affective taxonomy formulated by Krathwohl and others
2. Any interpretive assimilation of the correlative mode
3. The minimum essentials of valid behavioral objectives
4. The scope and focus of all pertinent socioeconomic factors
5. The componential perceptions affecting an integrative approach
6. The transitory utilization of polarized value judgments
7. Any conformation of preestablished divergent assumptions
8. The impetus of value indicators restructured through diverse areas of the continuum
9. Humanistic techniques of career orientation modeled after the Harmin-Simon approach
10. Nonsupportive and immediate response situations derived from key result areas

DISCUSSION

1. Do you know anyone who uses language that is similar to this? If so, who?
2. What causes people to use EMBS?
3. Does this type of language have any effect on society? If so, in what ways?

Facts do not cease to exist because they are ignored.
—*A. Huxley*

What Am I?
"I'm the beginning of eternity, the end of time and space,
the beginning of every end, the end of every place."
What am I?

REACTIONS TO CHAPTER 5

Answer the question assigned by your instructor. Remember, openness and honesty are the first steps to being a more effective communicator.

1. Select one of the language barriers to communication that you have experienced in your own communication. Describe the barrier, and indicate how it interfered with your communication. What skill will you use in the future to overcome the barrier?

2. In what ways does our reaction to words (semantic reactions) affect our communication?

3. What suggestions would you make to improve communication with respect to semantic reactions?

4. From the very beginning of the day, how long did it take you to slip and use a label or the stereotype someone? What was it? What should you have done?

5. If words have power, how is it that "words don't mean; people mean"?

6. Give a recent example of how you reacted to a word because of its connotative, rather than denotative, impact.

7. Give a recent example of sexism in your language. How might you rid your language behaviors of this barrier?

Understanding Self

◇ **Self-Image**

Definition: How we describe, picture, view ourselves. It is objective, describable, measurable, and checkable.

Example: "I am a black female, 24 years old, weighing 123 pounds, 5 feet 6 inches tall." Self-image changes slowly because we develop physically gradually and over extended periods of time.

◇ **Self-Esteem**

Definition: The value, worth, or importance that we put on what our self-image is. It is very subjective.

Example: "I like being black and female. I wish I were a bit older. I would like to lose 10 pounds. I like my height."

◇ **Self-Concept**

Definition: Our total or world view of ourselves. The complete picture including both our self-image and self-esteem.

Example: "I'm an attractive human being who is intelligent, who relates well to others, and who is generally successful in things I try." Our self-concept changes as our self-image or self-esteem is modified.

◇ **Role**

Definition: A part we are expected to play in our society.

Examples: Student, mother, brother, worker, athlete, consumer, woman/man, husband, girlfriend, citizen. We are expected to play hundreds of roles in our lives—the more complex our lives, the more roles we are expected to play.

◈ Performance Role

Definition: A role where we are paid (or receive some sort of remuneration) for meeting the role expectations as prescribed by the person or agency that "pays" us.

Example: As a student we meet the specifications set by our teacher. If we do so, we receive knowledge, grade, credit, and so on. As a worker we do what our boss tells us (often even dressing as directed); in return, we get a paycheck.

◈ Personality Role

Definition: A role where we have the right to determine the parameters of the role we are playing.

Example: Friend, brother, sex partner, woman, and so on. A son or daughter living at home with mom and dad paying the bills is in a performance role since the person is being "paid" her physical upkeep and therefore meets parents' expectations in doing chores around the house or being in at a certain time. However, when son/daughter moves out and begins paying his/her own bills, then son/daughter becomes a personality role.

◈ Role Expectations

The parameters or boundaries of the roles we are playing.

◈ Self-Disclosure

The process of communicating to others, verbally and nonverbally, our thoughts, feelings, attitudes, beliefs, and values. It is taking our masks off and revealing to another person our "real" self.

THE IMPORTANCE OF UNDERSTANDING SELF

- Who am I?
- How do I feel about myself?
- Do I like (or dislike) parts of my personality or physical appearance?
- Am I comfortable with myself?
- How can I improve my communication both with myself and with others?

These questions are asked by everyone at some time in life. Many of us are confused over the issues of who we really are and the roles we are expected to play to gain societal or peer acceptance. We are frustrated by the demands of people around us who want us to behave according to their expectations of us and our own expectations of who we are and what we want to be.

Is it possible to know and like who we are, to get in touch with the "real me" buried underneath all the roles we are expected to play in order to be a functioning part of our culture? If it is possible, do we really want to know ourselves? To know and to let others truly know us demands taking risks and being vulnerable. Is it "safer" to live our lives meeting others' expectations and keeping the "real" us hidden from view?

And what does all of this have to do with communication? This, after all, is a book about communication—not psychology.

Here are some things to think about—from people much wiser than the authors of this book.

Honore De Balzac, the great French philosopher-historian, wrote, "Nothing is a greater impediment to being on good terms with others than being ill at ease with yourself."

With regard to meeting the expectations of others, Rabbi Mendel of Kotzk wrote:

> *If I am because I am I,*
> *And you are you because you are you,*
> *Then I am, and you are*
> *But if I am I because you are you,*
> *And you are you because I am I,*
> *Then I am not, and you are not.*

Eleanor Roosevelt, one of the greatest women in American history, who survived a lifetime of people attempting to "put her down," wrote, "No one can make you feel inferior without your consent."

Some things to think about? We hope this chapter will give you some answers to the questions we have asked above—and the encouragement to find out and let others know who you really are.

BARRIERS TO UNDERSTANDING SELF

There are real barriers put in place by others and ourselves to our getting to know, accept, and like ourselves. Some of them are:

- Our confusion between the types of roles we play—those personality roles where we have the right to determine the way the role is played and those performance roles where others have the right to define some of the parameters.

- Our fear of risking letting others know what we are truly thinking and feeling because if we do "they" might not like us anymore.

- Our unwillingness to change. Even if where we are hurts, we sometimes view change as worse than the pain and loneliness we are currently feeling.

- Our practice of comparing ourselves with others—not recognizing that when we do that, we automatically make ourselves into losers.

- Our problems with accepting ourselves as we are—zits and all—learning that there are some things about ourselves that we cannot change, and that we might just as well learn to accept those things (and maybe like and use them!).

- Our false modesty that does not allow us to rejoice in our own uniqueness and to define, refine, and emphasize our strong qualities and attributes.

- Our failure to prescribe and follow plans that help us to change those things about ourselves that we can change and want to change.

MISS PEACH   By Mell Lazarus

Exercising Compliments

PURPOSE

To learn how to give compliments or do something nice for other people, and to record their reactions.

PROCEDURE

For this assignment, you are to give at least 10 compliments or actions to 10 different people. Below, list the person you addressed, what you said or did, and the reaction of the person receiving the compliment.

Person:
Compliment:
Reaction:

Person:
Compliment:
Reaction:

Person:
Compliment:
Reaction:

Person:
Compliment:
Reaction:

Person:
Compliment:
Reaction:

Person:
Compliment:
Reaction:

Person:
Compliment:
Reaction:

Person:
Compliment:
Reaction:

Person:
Compliment:
Reaction:

Person:
Compliment:
Reaction:

PURPOSE

To see how people respond to compliments.

PROCEDURE

1. Divide into groups of five or six people.
2. Select a recorder—a person who will write down everything that is said to a particular individual.
3. Starting anywhere in the circle, one person will be focused upon. Once selected, the group will then start giving compliments to the "focused" person. The best way to do this is to simply go around the circle a few times.
4. After the person has received at least 10 compliments the recorder will hand them the written account of what just transpired. Then another person is selected to be the focus individual. This process will continue until everyone has been focused upon.

DISCUSSION

1. How did you feel when you were the focus person?
2. Did you find it difficult to give compliments to other people?
3. Is giving compliments to other people a motivational skill?
4. In what aspects of your life can you employ what you did in this group?

"Who Are You?"
"Who are you?" said the caterpillar. Alice replied rather shyly, "I-I hardly know, sir, just at present—at least I know who I was when I got up this morning, but I must have changed several times since then." —*Lewis Carroll*

Turning Points in My Life

PURPOSE

To identify events in your life which have affected you and your intra/interpersonal communication.

PROCEDURE

1. In the space below, list at least 10 events in your life which could be said to have been turning points—i.e., travel experiences, school experiences, births, deaths, embarrassments, milestones, etc.

   a.

   b.

   c.

   d.

   e.

   f.

   g.

   h.

   i.

   j.

2. Briefly state how each of these affected you and your intra/interpersonal communication.
3. Once you have completed these, form small groups and discuss what each has written. Also, discuss the following questions.

DISCUSSION

1. Specifically, how have these events related to your own intra/interpersonal communication?
2. How might these events relate to the self-fulfilling prophecy, which states that people tend to become what they are told they are or think they are?
3. Are there any similar events which have affected people in your group? Discuss.
4. Do people of other cultures react differently from you to your turning points? How/why?

PURPOSE

To identify the feelings that each person is comfortable with and can express.

PROCEDURE

First, complete the survey below. Circle the number that expresses how well you deal with each feeling listed.

Rating Scale

1 Can express completely in any situation
2 Can express 75% of the time
3 Can express 50% of the time—with difficulty
4 Express only 25% of the time—with reservation
5 Do not express except on a very rare occasion

caring	1	2	3	4	5	displeasure	1	2	3	4	5
sharing	1	2	3	4	5	tension	1	2	3	4	5
love	1	2	3	4	5	hurt	1	2	3	4	5
liking	1	2	3	4	5	disappointment	1	2	3	4	5
concern	1	2	3	4	5	disgust	1	2	3	4	5
sadness	1	2	3	4	5	joy	1	2	3	4	5
depression	1	2	3	4	5	excitement	1	2	3	4	5
fear	1	2	3	4	5	pride	1	2	3	4	5
anger	1	2	3	4	5	patriotism	1	2	3	4	5

Complete the sentences below:

a. I am disgusted when _____

b. I get angry when _____

c. The thing that frightens me most is _____

d. Love is a feeling _____

e. To like someone is _____

f. I am disappointed with _____

g. I take pride in _____

h. I feel tense _____

i. I am concerned about _____

j. The last time I felt real joy was _____

k. I am excited about _____

l. The thing that hurts me most is _____

m. The thing that depresses me most frequently is _____

n. I very much care about _____

o. I enjoy sharing _____

p. I feel _____

q. Patriotism _____

r. I am displeased with _____

Form dyads and discuss your answers from the above.

DISCUSSION

1. What part do feelings play in verbal communication? In nonverbal communication?
2. Is there a feeling that you absolutely cannot deal with? If so, what?
3. How important are feelings to you?
4. How can you work on dealing more effectively with your feelings?
5. Which feeling do you think you deal with most successfully?
6. How do feelings affect your perception?

Everything that irritates us about others can lead us to an understanding of ourselves. —C. Jung

PURPOSE

To determine the nature of self-confidence, and how to increase it.

PROCEDURE

Next to each situation, rate how strong your self-confidence is, based on the rating scale.

Rating Scale

1 Feel completely self-confident and capable
2 Feel capable, but have some feelings of self-consciousness
3 Feel very self-conscious, but do an adequate job
4 Feel inferior to the point that it hampers my ambition, willingness to try, for fear of failure
5 Complete fear of failure—no self-confidence— will not try at all—don't get in these kinds of situations

_____ 1. In front of a group—acting as the leader

_____ 2. In sports (tennis, basketball, etc.)

_____ 3. In scholastic competition

_____ 4. In my looks

_____ 5. My ability to communicate

_____ 6. My ability to do my job

_____ 7. Taking on added responsibilities

_____ 8. Organizing a big program

_____ 9. As a husband/wife/boy friend/girl friend

_____ 10. Acting as the stabilizing factor

_____ 11. As a parent or a future parent

_____ 12. Artistic/creative abilities

_____ 13. Carry on a conversation

_____ 14. Going on an interview

_____ 15. Volunteering for demonstration

_____ 16. Entering a new situation—new group of people

_____ 17. Speaking out in a group of strangers

_____ 18. Ability to begin a task and carry it through

_____ 19. Risk-taking

_____ 20. Trusting others

DISCUSSION

1. Will your self-confidence affect your future success? If so, how?
2. Will it affect your interpersonal relationships? How?

I care not what others think of what I do, but I care very much about what I think of what I do: that is character!
—*T. Roosevelt*

Interpersonal Confidence Walk

PURPOSE

To examine the ways in which you gain interpersonal confidence or trust.

PROCEDURE

1. Your instructor will assign you a partner.
2. Have your partner blindfold you. She will take you around the room, building, or campus.
3. When the blindfolded partner has developed a high degree of confidence or trust, switch places and continue your walk.

RULES FOR TRUST WALK

1. Walk—**Don't run**.
2. Remain in body contact with your partner from the instant the blindfold goes on.
3. Talk to your partner. Share **thoughts** and **feelings**.
4. Remove blindfold and return to the classroom if any of the following happens:
   a. Your partner says she cannot continue.
   b. Your partner violates your trust **in any way**.
   c. Your partner becomes frightened, dizzy, or disoriented.
5. Follow the prescribed route.
6. After you have reversed roles, and both persons have been on the trust walk, thank each other and talk about your experience.

DISCUSSION

1. How long did it take you to develop confidence in your partner?
2. How was this confidence developed? Be specific.
3. Describe the communication between you and your partner during your walk.

> If you aspire to the highest place,
> it is no disgrace to stop at the second or even the third.
> —*M. Cicero*

Role Analysis

PURPOSE

To examine more closely the roles you play and how these roles affect aspects of communication.

PROCEDURE

Answer the following questions individually and then we will discuss the responses as a class.

1. Try to list five of the roles that you commonly play, making each role separate and distinct from the others—i.e., student, mother, wife, etc.

2. How are each of the following altered by each of the above roles?

    a. Language

    b. Appearance

    c. Attitude

    d. Values

    e. Quantity and quality of communication

3. What major role expectations do you have for each of the following roles?

a. Teacher

k. Clergyman

b. Student

1. Parishioner

c. Wife

m. Doctor

d. Husband

n. Patient

e. Boy friend

o. Policeman

f. Girl friend

p. Citizen

g. Mother

q. Employer

h. Father

r. Employee

i. Son

s. Clerk

j. Daughter

t. Customer

4. Analyze the following situations according to how different people might deal with them.

   a.   What questions might each person ask?

   b.   What factors would determine their reaction to each situation?

How would a . . .	deal with . . .
mother	buying a car
father	selecting a college
fashion model	seeing a ball game
preacher	going on vacation
boy friend	selling a boat
girl friend	stealing an orange
cab driver	punishing a small child
salesperson	getting a speeding ticket
police officer	going to the dentist
rich student	paying a fine
poor student	using leisure time

DISCUSSION

1. How do roles affect interpersonal communication?
2. Discuss role playing as a means of solving problems that occur in interpersonal communication situations.

The Johari Window provides a way to look at the self. There are things you know about yourself and things you don't know. There are things other people know about you and things they don't know. These four aspects represent the various areas of the self.

AREA 1, open area (I know, others know) represents your public self. The information is common knowledge and you feel free about sharing that information with others.

AREA 2, blind area (others know, I don't know) includes information others have about you, but that you do not have. This, for example, is the way you look to other people.

AREA 3, the hidden area (I know, others don't know) represents the things that you know about yourself, but have been unwilling to share with others. This area includes your secrets and things you are ashamed of.

AREA 4, the unknown area (I don't know, others don't know) represents those things about yourself that you don't understand. This is the area of needs, expectations, and desires you have that you cannot understand.

The four areas are interdependent, that is, a change in the size of one area affects the size of the other areas. By self-disclosing, an individual increases the free area and decreases the size of the hidden area. As a result of the hidden area being decreased, the unknown area is likewise decreased. Such disclosing on the part of an individual makes feedback easier by others and, therefore, the blind area and unknown area are also reduced in size.

Self-disclosure can then be seen as a means to aiding an individual in learning more about the self.

The Johari Window

Open Self	Blind Self
Hidden Self	Unknown Self

The Johari Window Exercise

PURPOSE

To examine the degree of overall "openness" of your communication.
To provide insight into the hidden areas of your personality.
To demonstrate self-disclosure as a situational variable.

PROCEDURE

Draw your Johari Window for each of the following environments: speech class, close family, friendship group, spouse, boy friend/girl friend.

DISCUSSION

How do the windows for each of the environments differ?

Maslow's Hierarchy of Needs

Maslow has classified the basic needs of man into five broad categories:

1. PHYSIOLOGICAL NEEDS—These are necessary for survival. They include the need for food, drink, shelter, sex, avoidance of injury, pain, discomfort, disease, or fatigue, and the need for sensory stimulation. If physiological needs are not satisfied, they are stronger in their motivation than any higher needs.

2. SAFETY NEEDS—These focus on the creation of order and predictableness in one's environment. They include preference for orderliness and routine over disorder, preference for the familiar over the unfamiliar.

3. LOVE NEEDS—These are of two types: love and affection between husband and wife, parents and children and close friends; and the need for belonging—identifying the larger groups (church, club, work, organization, etc.). When these needs are not met, feelings of rejection and isolation result with subsequent feelings of mistrust and suspicion toward others.

4. ESTEEM NEEDS—These refer to the desire for reputation, prestige, recognition, attention, achievement and confidence. Some sociologists believe that esteem needs are powerful motivators in America.

5. SELF-ACTUALIZATION—The fulfillment of one's capabilities and potentialities. Self-actualization needs take on strong motivating power only when other more basic needs have been fulfilled.

According to Maslow, higher needs act as motivating forces only when those preceding them on the hierarchy have been satisfied.

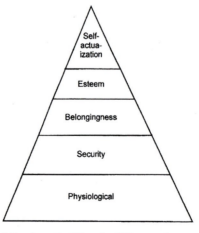

Maslow's Needs Hierarchy

Island Activity

PURPOSE

To help you understand and explore Maslow's theory of human motivation and how it relates to communication.

PROCEDURE

1. Read the following story and determine the order in which you would make your requests.
2. Form a small group and reach a group consensus on the order of the request.
3. After the groups have reached consensus, compare the groups' ranking with Maslow's hierarchy.

Situation

You are the sole survivor of your wrecked ship. You have been rescued by a wealthy and eccentric recluse who lives on an uncharted island somewhere in the South Pacific with a small group of his followers. Because the island is uncharted, there is no hope of rescue. Your host, who discovered the island years earlier with his small band of followers, has indicated that you are welcome and all your needs and wants will be satisfied—all you have to do is ask. Below are five requests that you may make. Place them in the order in which you would make them.

Individual	Group	
_____	_____	companionship of others
_____	_____	the ability to determine your goals and strive to achieve them
_____	_____	food, drink, shelter, sex
_____	_____	recognition and attention from others
_____	_____	a set of guidelines describing how life on the island is structured

DISCUSSION

1. How does your ranking and that of your group compare with Maslow's hierarchy?
2. Do you agree or disagree with Maslow's theory? Why?
3. Why do you think Maslow felt most Americans were at level 4?
4. Is there anything about our society that may keep a person from meeting their esteem needs?
5. How does a self-actualized person behave?
6. What role does communication play in meeting needs at each level?
7. What kind of communicator is a self-actualized person?
8. Using communication, how can you help a person move from level 4 to level 5?

REACTIONS TO CHAPTER 6

1. Is it possible to know and like who we are?

2. What does knowing who we are have to do with our communication skills?

3. Are the risks of revealing our "real selves" to others worth it? Why or why not?

4. What harm does role playing do to the communication process? When is it appropriate to play roles?

5. Is it true that we have to know and love ourselves before we can know and love others? Why or why not?

6. Are there any cautions to be observed when we are trying to be open and honest in our communication? If so, what are they?

Values

Valuing is one of our most precious personal rights. Yet it seems increasingly clear that all too few humans understand what they value. This chapter describes the process of "valuing," and helps participants to not only clarify their values, but ascertain the relationship of these values to the attitudes and behaviors that they exhibit. Do you always understand why you are making a decision, and on what principle it stands? Is your behavior consistent or inconsistent with what you say? Are you consistent in how you apply standards, expectations, or judgments from one person to the next?

In order to understand the relationship of values to behavior, attitudes, and perception, we first need to look at some basic definitions inherent to the discussion of values.

◆ **Values**

Long-enduring ideas of what is desirable, which influence choices from available possibilities for action.

◆ **Beliefs**

Our perceptions about reality that drive our attitudes.

◆ **Attitudes**

Our views about things that usually give direction to our behaviors.

◆ **Behaviors**

The acting out of our desires, fears, decisions; the process of making our body take some action in one direction or another—following up on our intentions—with action; to proceed with, discharge, enact, play one's part, conduct oneself.

◇ Attributes

Definition:

Those characteristics that define something—that by which it can be described and put into perspective against other things.

Example: Height, gender, personality, intelligence

◇ Consequences

Definition:

The possible outcomes of any given action(s).

Example: Break the law—pay the price.

◇ Choosing

Definition:

The act of placing in a higher priority one thing over another—the act of selection, picking, using discretion to select among alternatives.

Example: Selecting a life partner

◇ Preferences

Definition:

Those things that we place a higher priority on than on others; if we had our way and were free to choose, we would go with these things.

Example: All children will be safe and cared for.

◇ Decision Making

The process of:

1. clarifying the problem or choice,
2. gathering pertinent data,
3. identifying possible alternatives,
4. verifying the consequences of alternatives, and
5. choosing one alternative over the other.

◇ Judging

The process of evaluating someone, an action, or an outcome, on the basis of self-established criteria—the discrimination among options; the imposing of values on someone else; the process of estimating, awarding, reviewing, critiquing and reporting the conclusion thereof.

THE IMPORTANCE OF VALUES

Values are not just important in their own right. They serve as a base for decisions, actions, and judgments, and are crucial to making decisions. In those instances when an individual (or group) either knows or is able to explain her values related to the problem, she can use those values directly, deliberately, and openly in making the decision. In those instances in which the individual is unaware of her values, those values act at a subconscious level. That is, a plausible solution is that making the decision may be highly frustrating because there are competing values acting on the individual, but she is unaware of the source of conflict and thereby unable to respond to the real issue.

It is the purpose of this chapter to present information and exercises that will enable you, by the end of the chapter, to answer the following questions:

1.   What is a value?

2.   How do values relate to my everyday life?

3.   How do values affect the decision-making process?

4.   How are values formulated?

5.   How do values affect my interpersonal communication?

6.   What are factors that alter the existence of values in my life?

7.   How does "information" affect the valuing/decision-making process?

BARRIERS TO UNDERSTANDING VALUES

In our highly technological information society today, we are constantly being bombarded by conflicting opinions, views, beliefs, and desires of other people, groups, family, friends, and general public opinion. This information, and the influence with which it is displayed to us, present many potential barriers to actually developing clear values for ourselves.

Confusion often exists between what we were taught to believe as youngsters and what we believe as adults.

Think for a moment about what opinions and values you borrowed from your parents, and about those aspects of your current lifestyle that are similar to or very different from those of your family members. Think back on those cliches or traditions that you participated in and/or heard as a child that have affected you today.

All of us receive some of our values initially from our families; sometimes those values are based in our religion, nationality, race, socioeconomic status, and political upbringing. As we grow older, we sometimes re-examine the values that we "absorbed"—usually because a behavior facing us comes into conflict with our belief system.

Lack of Accurate Information

Ignorance for some is bliss . . . and it can allow us to not see the total picture. When we don't have as much relevant information as possible—when we have only seen one side versus all sides, and when certain key and relevant facts or perspectives are not known to us—we choose from what is known and the choice may, in the larger context, be inappropriate.

Personal Biases of Others That Have No Bearing in the Rational World

If we care about or admire someone, we tend to give their thoughts and feelings more credence and priority. Sometimes, because we do not want to offend people we care about, are close to, or are related to, we do not take the risk of offending them by "owning" values different from theirs.

Peer—Family—Work Pressure

All of us are subject to pressures from all of those around us. All of the avenues within which we function—family, work, social—have organizational cultures that reflect values. This culture, both directly and subtly, forces us to confront its values. The threats of noncompliance, rejection, and ostracism are usually present. And some of us are not comfortable with "being in the minority" in our thought—of not conforming and being part of whatever "normative" culture we are a part of.

Conflicting Values

At one time or another, we are all faced with alternatives to the decision process that are based on values that seem to conflict. For example, a person who has a priority on stability and security—who values his house and wants to stay there—may be faced with a job promotion that requires him to move somewhere else. Upward mobility and success may also be a high priority. But when placed against the security and stability of a house, which one will prevail?

Lack of Empowerment

People with self-confidence usually do not have any problem being able to articulate their values. They may change their values, but they feel empowered—they feel able to be in charge of the changes. A lack of this feeling—knowing that you are, and have a right to be, in control—can be a barrier in that you may not be able to exercise the control to identify for yourself and be comfortable with your choice.

Consistency

As choices emerge, in a variety of circumstances, especially if they include passing judgment on ourselves versus others, we sometimes have the tendency to be inconsistent in what values guide our decisions. But, if something is truly a value for us, should or shouldn't it apply to all circumstances?

Changing Circumstances

As circumstances and events change, so does pertinence of our decisions. We all must re-evaluate from time to time our choices based on emerging circumstances, and these can pose a challenge to our value system. If we value something because it has certain attributes—and the attributes change—what happens to how we feel about the value?

> The greatest discovery of my generation is that a human being can alter his life by altering his attitude.
> —W. James

Values Exercise

PURPOSE

To examine the basis for the things that we believe.

PROCEDURE

Form groups of 5–6 and answer the discussion questions below. Have one member record your group responses.

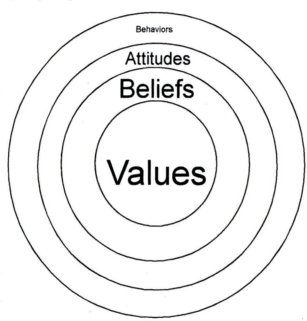

DISCUSSION

1. Define
   a. Value   c. Attitude
   b. Belief   d. Behavior
2. Where do values come from?
3. Is it possible to have a **belief** about something that is not supported by a **value**? How? Example?
4. Consider your feelings about taking an elective class in Music Appreciation. Trace those feelings from the attitude you have to the **belief** and ultimately the **value.** Can you do the same thing with your attitude about next Saturday's plans? Or your position on abortion?
5. Can we change our **values**? How? What effect would changing a **value** have on the rest of your life?

A Study of American Youth

PURPOSE

To explore how values may change from generation to generation.

PROCEDURE

Some contrasting highlights of student attitudes and values appear below. Look at the attitude/values chart below and, for each area, determine what the appropriate attitude/values are for the 2000s column, and fill those in.

1960s/1970s	1980s/1990s	2000s
The 1960s had been characterized by a lot of campus rebellion, which ceased in the 1970s.	Student awareness/change within the rules.	
New lifestyles and radical politics appear linked in the 1960s: commune living, pot smoking, long hair, and student protest marches. In the 1970s, almost total divorce between radical politics and new lifestyles.	Acceptance/tolerance of divergent lifestyles.	
In the 1960s, campus search for self-fulfillment in place of conventional career, which changed to a search for self-fulfillment with the career in the 1970s.	Movement toward financial security; interest in career secondary to financial gain.	
A growing criticism of our "sick" society in the 1960s had lessened by the 1970s.	Constructive criticism; active, informed opinions.	
In the 1960s, the Women's Movement had little impact on youth values and attitudes. In the 1970s, a wide and deep penetration of women's lib ideas.	Concept of equality accepted by a significant number of students.	

1960s/1970s	1980s/1990s	2000s
Violence on campus was condoned, romanticized in the 1960s, but was rejected in the 1970s.	Violence continues to be rejected.	
In the 1960s, the gap widened in values, morals, and outlook between young people and their parents, especially college youth. In the 1970s, the younger generation and older mainstream America moved closer in values, morals, and outlook.	Students aware of and interested in what parents and middle Americans believe.	
In the 1960s, a sharp split in social and moral values found within youth generation and between college students and the non-college majority. Gap within generation proves to be larger and more severe than gap between generations. In the 1970s, the gap within generation narrows: non-college youth virtually caught up with college students in new social and moral norms.	Gap between generations very narrow; gap between economic groups (college vs. disenfranchised) quite large.	
In the 1960s, challenge to traditional work ethic confined to campus. In the 1970s, work ethic strengthened on campus; growing weaker among non-college youth.	Work ethic continues to grow weaker.	

1960s/1970s	1980s/1990s	2000s
New code of sexual morality in the 1960s, centering on greater acceptance of casual premarital sex, abortion, homosexuality, and extra-marital relations, confined to minority of college students, spreads to mainstream of both college and working-class youth.	Sexual morality significantly affected by sexually trans-mitted diseases.	
Harsh criticism of major institutions, political parties, big business, military almost confined to college students in the 1960s. In the 1970s, criticism of some major insti-tutions tempered on campus, taken up by working-class youth.	Criticism reflects more enlightened, mature judg-ments.	
In the 1960s, campus was main focus of youthful dis-content. Non-college youth were quiet. In the 1970s, campuses were quiet. Many signs of latent discontent and dissatisfaction among work-ing-class youth.	Campuses reflect growing political/social involvement, but within the law.	
Much youthful energy and idealism devoted to concern with minorities. African-Americans considered most oppressed in the 1960s. In the 1970s, concern with minorities lower. Native Americans considered most oppressed.	Minority awareness very high on campus, even lead-ing to political action.	

1960s/1970s	1980s/1990s	2000s
In the 1960s, the college youth left or liberal. By the 1970s, no clear-cut political center; pressures from both right and left. New left and radicals decline.	Significant swing to conservative values and ideals.	
In the 1960s, law and order anathema to campus. In the 1970s, campus shows greater acceptance of law and order.	Law and order on campus is norm. Disorder is abnormal behavior.	

Adapted from *The New Morality* by Daniel Yankelvich

DISCUSSION

1. What general conclusions can you come to about how attitudes and values have changed over the above time period?
2. Why do you think these changes occur?
3. What changes might occur within the next decade?

One cannot have wisdom without living life. —*D. McCall*

The Lawrence Kohlberg Moral Development Scale

The Scale

1. Is universal, consistent, and unchanging—the world over!
2. Is inflexibly sequentially upwards (a person may be halfway in one stage and "spill over" in the neighboring two).
3. Focuses on *why* (the reason) a decision is made, not *what* the decision is (two people at differing stages on the scale can make the same decision—but for different reasons).
4. Is dependent on conflict (either direct or empathic) for upward growth.
5. Upper levels (5–6) demand high cognitive development, high intelligence, well educated).

Scale Level	Description	Behavioral Reasoning
1	Deference to authority	"I did it because _____ told me to."
2	Sense of satisfaction of own needs	"I did it because I wanted to."
3	Seeking approval through being "good" or "nice"	"I did it because _____ will approve of (like) me for making that choice."
4	Respect for law & order	"the rules are. . . . The law is. . . . The book says. . . ."
5	Societal needs	"what is the greatest good for the greatest number?" "Considering everybody involved, what is the best decision?"
6	Universal ethical principle	"I make my moral decisions based on a carefully thought out, personally chosen ethical standard that emphasizes the worth and dignity of life."

PURPOSE

To examine your position in moral maturity according to the Kohlberg scale.

PROCEDURE

1. Write down the last time you did something you **knew** was wrong. The more significant the issue, the more meaningful this lesson will be. Try to choose something that you had to **think** about. **Everybody** exceeds the speed limit. We often do it without any guilt at all, so pick something of **consequence.**
2. The issue may be one of ethics, morals, legality, or conduct.
3. You may be 100 percent honest. This assignment will **not** be turned in or shared with anyone else.
4. Identify (as close as you can) the reason(s) that best represents your justification to do the above-mentioned wrong (check all that apply).

    _____ A. "I was asked to, and I told 'em I would, so I went ahead and did it."
    _____ B. "My decision was really best for everyone involved."
    _____ C. "I know better than those who say `It's wrong'."
    _____ D. "It was a deal, I had to keep my word."
    _____ E. "Hey, I was told to do it. I had to do it."
    _____ F. "I was just doing my duty."
    _____ G. "Well, I could have gotten into trouble if I hadn't done it."
    _____ H. "Everybody else was doing it."
    _____ I. "I had a job to do and I did what I was supposed to do."
    _____ J. "I didn't want to disappoint anybody."
    _____ K. "My rules take precedence over other rules."

5. Your instructor will explain the concepts behind Moral Development and show you what level each item above corresponds to. Remember, this brief exercise is only an indication of your level; only **you** can accurately place yourself on the scale.

DISCUSSION

1. Does Kohlberg's scale fairly reflect Moral Development?
2. Do you agree with your "position" on the scale based on the exercise? Why?
3. What value to you as a communicator is this knowledge of your position?
4. What can you do to advance on Kohlberg's scale?

Complete the Thought

PURPOSE

To engage in free association and inductive reasoning in determining values you have.

PROCEDURE

1. Complete the following thoughts in the various sections.
2. Pair off and discuss your responses, letting someone else read yours first.
3. Discuss with your partner the "I" thoughts you like most and why.
4. Resume in a large group to share responses and answer discussion questions.

IN GENERAL

1. When it rains, I . . .
2. Crowded, bustling places make me feel . . .
3. In my spare time, I . . .
4. Abortion is . . .
5. Sex before marriage . .   .
6. As a societal institution, marriage . . .
7. Homosexuals . . .
8. Marijuana . . .
9. Minority groups in this country . . .
10. To me, money . . .

PERSONAL THOUGHTS

1. I cry when . . .
2. I feel most comfortable in a small group when . . .
3. People bother me when . . .
4. I feel self-conscious . . .
5. I am warm and sincere . . .
6. I get angry . . .
7. Religion is . . .
8. The out-of-doors makes me feel . . .
9. The mountains make me aware . . .
10. Ocean waves remind me of . . .

11. The beach is a place that . . .

12. If I had 6 months to live, I would . . .

13. My mother . . .

14. My father . . .

15. The quiet activity I enjoy most is . . .

16. The sport that interests me the most is . . .

17. The most influential person in my life has been . . .

18. More than anyone else, I respect . . .

19. The single most motivational *factor* or event in my life was . . .

20. If I could change one thing about myself, I would . . .

21. The thing I like most about myself is . . .

22. I feel very inferior when . . .

23. The situation I feel most secure in is . . .

24. Of all the many faces of myself, I like the role of . . .

25. Psychological, emotional, relational game-playing is something that . . .

26. Most of all, I want to . . .

27. What I like least about myself is . . .

28. The physical characteristic about me that I like most is . . .

29. Intellectually, I . . .

30. I make myself laugh when I . . .

DISCUSSION

1. What, if anything, did you learn about yourself?
2. What values did you become aware of or reaffirm?
3. Are you a very social person, or private?
4. Did you find this hard to do? Why/why not?

Self-Appraisal

PURPOSE

To look at the ways you relate to others and the values behind your behavior. The form was originally developed by Edgar Schein, Bernard Bass, and James Vaughan. On the basis of this form you may analyze the way in which your values affect the manner in which you relate to others.

PROCEDURE

For each of the statements below, circle the number that best describes your place on the scale. Next, draw a diamond around the number that best expresses where you would like to be.

1. Ability to listen to others in an understanding way.

    Not at all able 1 2 3 4 5 6 7 8 9 10 Completely able

2. Willingness to discuss feelings with others.

    Not at all willing 1 2 3 4 5 6 7 8 9 10 Completely willing

3. Awareness of feelings of others.

    Not at all aware 1 2 3 4 5 6 7 8 9 10 Completely aware

4. Understanding why I do what I do.

    No understanding 1 2 3 4 5 6 7 8 9 10 Complete understanding

5. Tolerance of conflict and antagonism.

    Not at all tolerant 1 2 3 4 5 6 7 8 9 10 Completely tolerant

6. Acceptance of expressions of affection and warmth among others.

    Uncomfortably 1 2 3 4 5 6 7 8 9 10 Readily

7. Acceptance of comments about my behavior from others.

    Rejecting 1 2 3 4 5 6 7 8 9 10 Welcoming

8.   Willingness to trust others.

Completely suspicious 1 2 3 4 5 6 7 8 9 10 Completely trusting

9.   Ability to influence others.

Completely unable 1 2 3 4 5 6 7 8 9 10 Completely able

10. Relations with peers.

Wholly competitive 1 2 3 4 5 6 7 8 9 10 Completely able

DISCUSSION

1.   Identify which area you plan to concentrate on first to improve your communication.
2.   How must your change improve your communication?

Be the inferior of no man, nor of any man be the superior. Remember that every man is a variation of yourself. No man's guilt is yours, nor is any man's innocence a thing apart. Despise evil and ungodliness, but not men of ungodliness and evil.
—W. Saroyan

Lost in a Lifeboat!

You are aboard a luxury liner in the middle of the Pacific Ocean. As dusk approaches, you hear an alert signal to abandon ship. Passengers pour onto the lifeboats, but many do not clear ship before a bomb explodes and kills hundreds, completely destroying everything on the ship. The remainder of the ship sinks. You are in a lifeboat with 15 people; your boat is equipped to transport 8. You have only enough water for 10 people for 3 days. You must put 5 people into the water. Assume the 5 will go willingly but they cannot hang onto the side of the boat.

To aid in your decision, rank the people from 1–15, with 1 being the most necessary person to stay and 15 being the first person to go. You must exclude yourself from the decision. YD = your decision.

Now form a small group and develop a unanimous group ranking. GD = Group decision.

YD	GD		
_____	_____	1.	Minister, age 25, single, male, has a calming effect.
_____	_____	2.	Electrical engineer, 40s, female, only one able to fix the radio, if it can be fixed.
_____	_____	3.	Olympic swimmer, 40s, male, good organizer.
_____	_____	4.	Doctor, married, 3 children at home, age 35. Stole food from your food supply on the lifeboat with intention of keeping it for herself.
_____	_____	5.	Artist, male, 60, widowed, able to tell stories to keep spirits up.
_____	_____	6.	Navy captain, retired, age 70, divorced, blinded in explosion.
_____	_____	7.	Nurse, married, no children, female, age 30, tends toward hysteria.
_____	_____	8.	Pregnant lady, unmarried, age 27, illegal alien, was a prostitute.
_____	_____	9.	Teenage boy, Mexican-American, age 13, epileptic, gang member.

_____ _____ 10. Rabbi, male, age 40, has had a survival course.

_____ _____ 11. A campus militant, black, age 21, female, home economics major, on bail while on trial for terrorist activities.

_____ _____ 12. Scientist, Iraqi marine biologist, married with 2 kids, age 36, refuses to stay if rabbi stays.

_____ _____ 13. Youngster, male, age 7, only child, parents killed in explosion.

_____ _____ 14. Housewife, 45 years old, married, 2 children, can't swim, constant complainer.

_____ _____ 15. Ex-con, 31 years old, armed robbery, male, unmarried, 2 children, white, only one able to set the sail on the life boat, strong, member of the Aryan Brotherhood while in prison, crewed on an America's Cup sailboat 10 years ago.

DISCUSSION

1. On what values were your decisions based? Your group's decisions?
2. Did your values remain the same throughout, or did they change under peer pressure?
3. What further implications does this activity have for you in the real world?

REACTIONS TO CHAPTER 7

1. List three reasons why an understanding of values can help you be a more effective communicator.

   a.

   b.

   c.

2. If values are learned, why are they so difficult to change?

3. Identify the most significant event in your experience that caused you to evaluate a value. What was the outcome of that evaluation? How did it affect your beliefs? Your decisions? Your life?

4. What effect will an understanding of values have the next time you face an ethical decision? Do we always try to do what is "right"? Why?

Managing Conflict

The subject of conflict introduces some interesting dichotomies into the study of human communication. While the existence of conflict is a fact of life, we tend to treat conflict, whenever and wherever it is encountered, as something bad that should be avoided, sometimes at all costs. We therefore doom ourselves and our interactions to a nonproductive, negative cycle of avoidance and denial. This view of conflict generally arises, not so much from the conflicts themselves, but rather from the ways in which we try to manage, or more accurately, avoid managing them. In fact, it will be the contention of this chapter that conflict is neither good nor bad. It simply is! It is our preconceptions and ways of confronting conflicts that cause not only our overall negative attitude about them but also the nonproductive ways in which we attempt to manage them.

THE NATURE OF CONFLICT

In order to begin a better and more constructive outlook toward conflict, let's begin by understanding that conflict is really not a thing. Rather, conflict is a condition. It is a state of imbalance existing within an individual. Later we will consider the reason for the imbalance and the different types of conflict. But in order to see better what conflict is, it is necessary to define it.

By now, it is no surprise to you that many concepts in communication do not have a common, agreed-upon definition. As with the definition of communication itself, conflict has almost as many definitions as there are people to define it. However, for our purposes, let's consider a working definition.

A Definition

Conflict may be defined as *the perception of two or more, apparently mutually exclusive, objectives, choices, or courses of action that motivates the person, or persons, to seek to resolve the situation.* To begin to understand more about the nature of conflict, let us look more closely at the above definition. First of all, as was mentioned earlier, conflict is a condition—the perception of a situation. As soon as we label conflict a perception, we should remember what we have already learned about the process of perception, namely, that it is a highly subjective, incomplete, and inaccurate process that has been learned.

Therefore, our perceptions of conflicts are always going to carry these subjective, incomplete, and inaccurate traits. Furthermore, it matters little to attempt to prove or disprove in some objective sense whether or not a conflict really exists, as one might try to prove or disprove who won the Super Bowl in a given year. The perception that a conflict exists makes it real to the person or persons sharing that perception, and that is where we must begin—with that perception.

This perception has some special qualities about it that get us closer to an understanding of the nature of conflict. It is the element of exclusivity that begins to lead us down the path toward feeling or experiencing conflict. The idea here is based on one generally agreed principle of communication and psychology: Humans prefer a state of balance—a consistency within ourselves, our beliefs, our attitudes, and our view of the world. Just as we seek to maintain or restore this balance, we seek to avoid or eliminate imbalance.

An example might be helpful here. If I have two good friends who like me and also like each other, I can be said to be in a state of balance in this situation. However, if these two friends suddenly begin to dislike each other, I begin to experience imbalance. Or perhaps to put the example somewhat differently, what would happen if you were engaged to be married to someone but your parents, presumably people you like, dislike your future mate? We have all probably been in some kind of situation where this kind of imbalance existed and it is precisely this imbalance and the discomfort associated with it that motivate us to seek to resolve the situation, or, as we are defining it, the conflict.

This imbalance need not involve our feelings for people; this same condition can be prompted by having to choose between two equally appealing alternatives such as two or more places to go on vacation, items to order from the menu at your favorite restaurant, or two dates for the same evening. The issue is the same: Which do I choose? At this moment, I am in a conflict. Granted, some of these conflicts are quickly and easily resolved, but others can exist for long periods of time and cause us to be miserable. But in each, the goal is the same: to eliminate the imbalance in our perceptions.

One way to eliminate the imbalance is to make the choice, if choice is involved in the situation. Another way to manage the conflict is to have the imbalance resolved by another person or by the situation itself. For instance, if I am applying for a new job, there is a natural conflict occurring between me and all the other applicants for that same position. Once the choice has been made by the employer, that conflict is over. Sometimes another conflict surfaces, as we shall see a bit later on, but the specific conflict over who will be chosen will cease to exist.

Another way to eliminate a conflict is to discover that our perception is wrong, that is, that the items in apparent conflict are not really mutually exclusive. I don't have to choose between steak and lobster, I can order a combination of the two!

Still another approach is to separate the conflict items altogether by simply realizing that no balance can be achieved or perhaps even expected. In this situation, we can simply agree to disagree. This last situation is most often the case when people encounter conflicts with one another involving their values. If I like jazz and my wife likes opera, is it reasonable for us to try to resolve this apparent conflict? In fact, I am perhaps not even likely to view this situation as a conflict unless I take the position that there is only one type of music that both of us can like.

The Recipe Approach:

One way to look at the nature of conflict, and the nature of conflict management in particular, is to view the above definition as though it were a recipe. Each element of the definition is an ingredient which, when combined together, makes conflict. Therefore, all I have to do is eliminate one of the ingredients and I no longer have a conflict. This may seem overly simplistic but it is at the heart of productive conflict management.

CHARACTERISTICS OF CONFLICT

We have already discussed one of the essential characteristics of conflict—it is a *condition,* not a thing. However, there are several other characteristics that would be helpful to understand at this point. First, conflicts are generally neither productive nor nonproductive. Rather, it is the ways in which they are approached and managed that make the outcomes either productive or nonproductive.

Second, conflicts can be experienced *intrapersonally* or *interpersonally.* While it is true that as perceptions, all conflicts are really intrapersonal, to whatever extent that you and I share a similar perception of a conflict in which we perceive ourselves, it can be said that we are involved in an interpersonal conflict. It is important to be able to distinguish between these two in order to know how to go about resolving or managing the conflict. I cannot resolve an interpersonal conflict on my own. I must resolve it interpersonally. It is also important to recognize when I am experiencing an intrapersonal conflict. It is often the case that individuals misanalyze a conflict and attempt to deal with an intrapersonal conflict as if it were really an interpersonal one, resulting in behaviors that attempt to put blame on others rather than realizing that the conflict and the resolution of it rest with us.

A third characteristic of conflict deals with its structure or context. In this sense we can classify conflict as either formal or informal. *Formal* conflict is characterized by rules, an acknowledged structure such as time limits, order of presentation of arguments, and so on, and usually by the fact that a third party usually determines the resolution of the conflict. Conflicts involving the courtroom, ballot box, and debating area are types of formal conflict. The important thing with these types of conflicts is to understand the structure and rules and to realize that the other person or opponent is not the one to be convinced but rather the third party. I have often judged intercollegiate debates in which the conflicting sides tried endlessly to convince one another of the correctness of their own viewpoint, while ignoring the fact that I was the one who would ultimately decide who won!

Informal conflicts, on the other hand, have no formal rules or structure and the resolution must come from the ones in conflict. These are the ones in which we find ourselves daily and that usually present the most challenge. If you and I are in a conflict and it is up to us to come to mutual agreement as to its resolution, our communication skills are truly put to the test. We cannot turn to others to decide for us; we cannot appeal to some unseen judge; we must rely on each other and ourselves.

TYPES OF CONFLICT

With the above concepts in mind, let's examine the kinds of conflicts that can occur, and how they can be characterized according to the above classifications. Conflicts can generally be classified into one of the following seven categories:

1. Content

2. Decisional

3. Material

4. Role

5. Judgmental

6. Expectancy

7. Ego

Content conflicts arise over perceived differences in facts or information. For example, if you and I are in a conflict over who won the Super Bowl in a given year, we are experiencing a "content" conflict. This type of conflict is almost always interpersonal. It can be either formal, as in the case of whether or not a defendant is guilty, or informal, as in the case of who won the Super Bowl. Content conflicts are perhaps the easiest to resolve, in that all that is needed is more information or a re-examination of existing information. There is generally little room for compromise here. The attempt is to determine who is right.

Decisional conflicts revolve around decisions that an individual or individuals must face. Sometimes these decisions involve simply ourselves and can therefore be classified as intrapersonal. In this case the conflicts often arise from alternatives that appear equally attractive or unattractive. A decision over which car to buy can confront an individual with equally attractive alternatives. On the other hand, a decision over whether to quit your job and risk unemployment or stay in your job and continue to be dissatisfied would be an example of equally unattractive alternatives. In either case, the approach toward resolution is the same—resolve the conflict by unbalancing the alternatives. In this case it is important to be honest with yourself regarding your feelings and to be as thorough as possible in investigating the alternatives.

The important steps in this process are to identify the alternatives, to evaluate each along with the outcomes each is likely to produce, and then to role-play the option you are considering taking. Acting as if you have made the decision in a particular way will allow you to see how the decision "feels." This will help you discover how easy it will be to live with the decision once you actually make it. It is also important to realize that few decisions, even once they are made, are irrevocable. If a decision turns out to be wrong, it is better to recognize that fact and then change it than to continue to live with the stress and dissatisfaction of a decision with which you are unhappy.

Interpersonal decisional conflicts simply compound the variables. Now more than one person's feelings and reactions must be considered. The steps, however, remain the same. Analyze, evaluate, and role-play the decision to determine how it feels. It is virtually impossible to live emotionally with a decision made on purely rational grounds. In the case of interpersonal conflicts of this type it is also important to look for compromise alternatives that may be more satisfactory to all parties.

Material conflicts are exclusively interpersonal, and involve competition for a limited resource, such as money, a job, property, food, or any other limited resource. The more of a limited resource one person gets, the less there is for someone else. The first step in dealing with this type of conflict is to determine if the resource in conflict is really limited. People often find themselves competing for things that are actually not in limited supply. Conflicts over love or esteem are examples of this misinterpretation. Once the resource has been determined to actually be in limited supply, it is then important for the parties in conflict to seek a "win-win" solution so that each leaves the conflict with more than they had previously but less than if there had actually been a "winner" and a "loser." "Win-lose" solutions invariably result in hard feelings and a desire on the part of the "loser" to get back at the other person the next time. When this occurs, such damage is done to the relationship that "win-lose" conflicts usually disintegrate into "lose-lose" conflicts.

Role conflicts are another type of conflict. These involve disagreements in role expectations between two people, or conflicting role expectations in the case of intrapersonal role conflict. As with decisional conflict, the steps to resolve this type of conflict involve a thorough analysis of the role expectations in conflict, a willingness to be open and honest about these expectations, and a willingness to negotiate a "win-win" solution. Couples having conflicts over their expectations of one another's behavior are prime examples of role conflicts. Sometimes the intervention of a third party, such as a marriage counselor, is necessary to encourage people to identify their expectations of one another and freely share those expectations with the other person. It is important here for an individual to be assertive and to be a "clean fighter."

The remaining three types of conflicts—*judgmental, expectancy,* and *ego*—are always destructive. *Judgmental* conflicts revolve around conflicting value statements as to the worth of something. Conflicts about whether or not a particular movie, book, or political candidate is good or bad are examples of this type of destructive conflict. In managing these conflicts it is important to remember that value judgments reflect an individual's value system and will always be to some degree different between people. Rather than continue to fight over whose judgment is correct, it is far more productive to acknowledge the right of each person to feel the ways he or she does and simply "agree to disagree." Once a person adopts this position, the alternatives are no longer mutually exclusive and, as stated earlier in this article, once we remove one of the elements in the definition of what conflict is, we no longer have conflict.

Expectancy conflicts are intrapersonal in nature, and deal with the expectations we set regarding the things and people in our world. It is a natural part of living to make expectations about people and situations, but if these expectations are unrealistic, the "reality" can never measure up and we doom ourselves to increasing amounts of dissatisfaction with life. Statements such as "that's not fair" or "that shouldn't have happened" are symptomatic of expectancy conflict. To deal more productively with our expectations it is important to try to perceive the world as accurately as possible and to realize that statements about the fairness or unfairness, or incorrectness of some happening ignore the reality that life is not fair nor correct; it simply is.

Finally, *ego* conflicts are the last type of conflict in which an individual can find himself or herself. These are the most destructive of all conflicts and can cause the most damage to relationships. In this type of conflict, the competition is over which person is the better person. Once our ego defense mechanisms come into play, good communication goes out the window and people begin attacking each other. There is no hope for resolution here. The rule is simply not to get into arguments over the worth of yourself compared to someone else. The unfortunate thing is that other types of conflicts often escalate into ego conflicts if they are not correctly identified and dealt with in a productive way. It is important here to learn to recognize "dirty fighting" behaviors, avoid using them yourself, and avoid others who insist on using them.

In order to begin to deal constructively with our conflicts it is important to first come to grips with what is in conflict; that is, what are the mutually exclusive objectives? Once these can be determined, applying the appropriate skills will lead to constructive and productive behaviors. Another valuable question to ask is "Who owns the conflict?" Many times we inadvertently buy into someone else's conflict and begin to think that it is actually ours. This mistake can doom us to frustration, since we cannot resolve a conflict to which we are not actually a party.

Now that we have examined in general what conflict is, and discussed the different types of conflict along with various characteristics of it, let's look at some of the barriers to handling conflict productively.

BARRIERS TO CONFLICT MANAGEMENT

Some barriers to managing conflict in a productive way are:

- **Avoidance**—As was mentioned at the outset, people tend to have a negative attitude about conflict and therefore tend to avoid dealing with conflicts once they are perceived, hoping that the conflict will simply go away.

- **Nonassertiveness**—Not being willing to speak your own mind and allow others the same opportunity increases frustration and distorts communication.

- **Misanalysis**—Buying into someone else's conflict or failing to analyze what is actually in conflict causes inappropriate behavior and may cause us to apply the wrong management strategy. Not being able to correctly determine who owns the problem is also an example of misanalysis.

- **Escalation**—Becoming defensive and thereby escalating the situation to an ego conflict produces disastrous effects.

- **Dirty fighting**—Using strategies associated with nonassertive, passive-aggressive, or aggressive behavior promotes poor communication and leads to escalation.

- **Competing**—Failing to recognize that interpersonal conflict management requires cooperation and good will between the parties generally brings about competition among the individuals involved in a conflict. Rather than cooperatively seeking a "win-win" solution, people go after a "win-lose" answer and ultimately everyone loses.

By understanding the true nature of conflict, developing a positive outlook about it, learning to recognize the types of conflicts in which we find ourselves, and avoiding destructive types of conflicts and the barriers to effective conflict management, we can begin to deal with our conflicts in a far more constructive and productive manner.

You cannot shake hands with a clenched fist. *—I. Gandhi*

Conflict Quiz

PURPOSE

To explore people's ideas regarding conflict

PROCEDURE

Indicate either "True" or "False" for each statement below.

True or False

_____ 1. Whenever conflict occurs, it's likely to be because there has been a misunderstanding.

_____ 2. As a general rule, it is better to avoid conflicts.

_____ 3. Conflicts always occur interpersonally.

_____ 4. Running a race is an example of conflict.

_____ 5. Assertive people are always trying to get their own way.

_____ 6. Nonassertive people don't experience conflicts.

_____ 7. You cannot resolve a conflict when you are angry.

_____ 8. Good communicators should be able to solve every conflict they encounter.

_____ 9. It's possible to be in a conflict and not know it.

_____ 10. Conflicts always end with a "winner" and a "loser."

DISCUSSION

1. Form a small group and compare your answers with one another.
2. What general ideas does your group have about regarding conflict?
3. Do these general ideas suggest any potential problems for dealing with conflict?

Feelings about Conflict

PURPOSE

To allow you to examine how we feel about conflicts.

PROCEDURE

Identify a recent conflict you have had.

1. What was it about?

2. Who was it with?

3. How did you handle it?

4. How satisfied are you with the results?

General feelings about conflict.

5. How do you feel when you know you are facing a conflict situation?

6. When you come away from a conflict feeling as though you *won,* how do you feel?

7. When you come away from a conflict feeling as though you *lost,* how do you feel?

8. When you experience a conflict that is not resolved, how do you feel?

9. Generally, when you experience a conflict, what do you do?

DISCUSSION

1. Form a small group and compare your responses to the above questions.
2. What general conclusions can you make about people's feelings regarding conflict?
3. What, if any, barrier to resolving conflicts can these feelings produce?

Identifying Conflicts Activity

PURPOSE

To help you identify the types of conflict we encounter in our daily lives.

PROCEDURE

Following is a list of the seven types of conflict discussed at the beginning of this chapter. For each example, write which type you think it is, in the space provided.

CONFLICT TYPES

CONTENT—disagreement over "facts"
DECISIONAL—decision about different courses of action to take
MATERIAL—competition for material goods such as money, job, etc.
ROLE—disagreement over role expectations and/or behavior
JUDGMENTAL—disagreement over the value or worth of something
EXPECTANCY—difference between our expectations of something and the
          perceived reality
EGO—disagreement over the worth of yourself or someone else

EXAMPLES

1. You are disagreeing with your boy friend/girl friend over which movie to see. _____

2. You are arguing with your brother or sister over who gets use of the family car on Friday night. _____

3. Your boss and you disagree about how you should act around the other employees in your area of responsibility. _____

4. You have had plans for a vacation in Hawaii for several months. You have arrived and now feel upset at how it is turning out. _____

5. You and your father or mother are having an argument over what time you need to be home from a date. _____

6. You are having a disagreement with a friend over who won the Oscar for Best Picture in 1988. _____

7. You are having an argument with a co-worker about the new sick leave policy that has been enacted. _____

8. You have decided to show another player on the team that you are better than him/her. _____

9. You are having a disagreement with your instructor about your study habits. _____

10. You and another employee are competing for the same promotion.

DISCUSSION

1. Compare your answers with others in the group.
2. As you identified these conflict types, what personal examples did you think of?

CRAZYMAKERS

What's your conflict style? To give you a better idea of some unproductive ways you may be handling your conflicts, we will describe some typical conflict behaviors that can weaken relationships. In our survey we will follow the fascinating work of Dr. George Bach, a leading authority on conflict and communication.

Bach explains that there are two types of aggression: clean fighting and dirty fighting. Because they either cannot or will not express their feelings openly and constructively, dirty fighters sometimes resort to "crazymaking" techniques to vent their resentments. Instead of openly and caringly expressing their emotions, crazymakers (often unconsciously) use a variety of indirect tricks to get at their opponent. Because these "sneak attacks" don't usually get to the root of the problem, and because of their power to create a great deal of hurt, crazymakers can destroy communication. Let's take a look at them.

The Avoider

The avoider refuses to fight. When a conflict arises, he will leave, fall asleep, pretend to be busy at work, or keep from facing the problem in some other way. This behavior makes it very difficult for the partner to express his feelings of anger or hurt, because the avoider won't fight back. Arguing with an avoider is like trying to box with a person who won't even put up his gloves.

The Pseudo-Accommodator

Not only does the pseudo-accommodator refuse to face up to a conflict, but she also pretends that there is nothing at all wrong. This really drives the partner—who definitely feels there is a problem—crazy, and causes that person to feel both guilt and resentment toward the accommodator.

The Guilt Maker

Instead of saying straight out that he doesn't want or approve of something, the guilt maker tries to change the partner's behavior by making that person feel responsible for causing pain. The guilt maker's favorite line is, "It's OK, don't worry about me. . . ," accompanied by a big sigh.

The Subject Changer

Really a type of avoider, the subject changer escapes facing up to aggression by shifting the conversation whenever it approaches an area of conflict. Because of these tactics, the subject changer and the partner never have the chance to explore their problem and do something about it.

The Criticizer

Rather than come out and express feelings about the object of her dissatisfaction, the criticizer attacks other parts of the partner's life. Thus, she never has to share what is really on her mind and can avoid dealing with painful parts of relationships.

The Mind Reader

Instead of allowing a partner to honestly express feelings, the mind reader goes into character analysis, explaining what the other person really means or what's wrong with the other person. By behaving this way the mind reader refuses to handle her own feelings and leaves no room for her partner to express himself.

The Trapper

The trapper plays an especially dirty trick by setting up a desired behavior for his partner, and then when it is met, attacking the very thing he requested. An example of this technique is for the trapper to say, "Let's be totally honest with each other," and then when the partner shares his feelings, he finds himself attacked for having feelings that the trapper doesn't want to accept.

The Crisis Tickler

This person almost brings what is bothering her to the surface, but she never quite comes out and expresses herself. Instead of admitting her concern about the finances she innocently asks, "Gee, how much did that cost?," dropping a rather obvious hint but never really dealing with the crisis.

The Gunnysacker

This person does not respond immediately when he is angry. Instead he puts his resentment into his gunnysack, which after a while begins to bulge with large and small gripes. Then, when the sack is about to burst, the gunnysacker pours out all his pent-up aggressions on the overwhelmed and unsuspecting victim.

The Trivial Tyrannizer

Instead of honestly sharing his resentments, the trivial tyrannizer does things he knows will upset his partner: leaving dirty dishes in the sink, clipping his fingernails in bed, belching out loud, turning up the television too loud, and so on.

The Joker

Because she is afraid to face conflicts squarely, the joker kids around when her partner wants to be serious, thus blocking the expression of important feelings.

The Beltliner

Everyone has a psychological "beltline," and below it are subjects too sensitive to be approached without damaging the relationship. Beltlines may have personality traits a person is trying to overcome. In an attempt to "get even" or hurt his partner, the beltliner will use his intimate knowledge to hit below the belt, where he knows it will hurt.

The Blamer

The blamer is more interested in finding fault than in solving a conflict. Needless to say, she usually does not blame herself. Blaming behavior almost never solves a conflict and is an almost surefire way to make the receiver defensive.

The Contract Tyrannizer

This person will not allow his relationship to change from the way it once was. Whatever the agreements the partner had as to roles and responsibilities at one time, they will remain unchanged. "It is your job to . . . feed the baby, wash the dishes, discipline kids, etc."

The Kitchen Sink Fighter

This person is so named because in an argument she brings up things that are totally off the subject ("everything but the kitchen sink"): the way her partner behaved last New Year's Eve, the unbalanced checkbook, bad breath—anything.

The Withholder

Instead of expressing her anger honestly and directly, the withholder punishes her partner by keeping back something—courtesy, affection, good cooking, humor, sex. As you can imagine, this is likely to build up even greater resentments in the relationship.

The Benedict Arnold

This character gets back at his partner by sabotage, by failing to defend her from attackers, and even by encouraging ridicule or disregard from outside the relationship.

Nonproductive Conflict Styles

PURPOSE

To help you explore the nonproductive ways we manage conflict.

PROCEDURE

1. Read the following descriptions of nonproductive styles, and try to identify those of which you may be guilty.
2. Form groups and answer the discussion questions below. Indirect conflicts often result in games because the individuals involved do not openly and directly acknowledge the real conflict. These games are called "crazymakers" or "dirty fights" by George Bach and they lead to a worsening of the conflict rather than to a satisfactory solution. There are three basic "crazymakers" styles:

   A. ***The Avoider.*** This person denies the conflict by refusing to face up to it directly and assertively.

   Typical Behaviors:
   * pretending there is nothing wrong
   * refusing to fight (falling asleep, leaving, pretending to be busy)
   * changing the subject whenever conversation approaches the area of conflict

- hinting at the conflict or talking in generalities but never quite coming out and expressing self

- kidding around when another person wants to be serious, thus blocking expression of important feelings

- attacking other parts of other person's life rather than dealing with real problem

B. ***The Manipulator.*** This person wants to "win." She attempts, in an indirect way, to get the other person to behave as she wants them to, rather than dealing in a direct way.

Typical Behaviors:

- trying to change other person's behavior by making them feel guilty or responsible ("It's OK, don't worry about me . . .")

- going into character analysis by explaining what's wrong with the other person or what the other person really means rather than allowing them to express themselves directly

- refusing to allow the relationship to change from what it once was

C. ***The Avenger.*** This aggressive behavior often results from nonassertive behavior. Because of an unwillingness to deal with the conflict openly and directly, this person attempts to get back at the other person in a number of indirect ways. An especially dirty fighter, he creates fights because he experiences second-order conflicts for which he wants to "pay back" or get even.

Typical Behaviors:

- storing up resentment and dumping it all on the other person all at once

- doing things to upset them

- finding fault by blaming other person for things

- bringing up things in an argument that are totally off the subject (other behavior, bad breath, etc.)

- attempting to punish partner by withholding

- encouraging others to ridicule or disregard partner

DISCUSSION

1. Which of the preceding styles have you been guilty of?
2. What were your feelings when employing any of these styles?
3. What were the results when you used these styles?

REACTIONS TO CONFLICT

As we have seen, there are various types of conflict, depending on the issue or issues involved as well as on whether the resolution must be intrapersonal or interpersonal. What we will now consider are the five ways that we may react to a conflict situation. The five types of reactions are:

- passively
- non-assertively
- aggressively
- passive-aggressively
- assertively

We will consider examples of each, along with typical behaviors associated with each.

Passively

While many articles tend to lump passive reactions together with non-assertive reactions, it is helpful for us to draw a distinction between the two. To react *passively* is to literally not experience any conflict with regard to a given situation. You do not experience any *imbalance* as we have presented previously. For example, if someone cuts in front of you while you are standing in line at a movie theater and it doesn't bother you, you are reacting *passively*.

While passive behavior appears the same as *non-assertive* behavior, it is important to consider what is happening inside of us in order to see the difference. Literally, to react passively is to not *experience* any conflict. In other words, the situation or issue just doesn't bother you.

Non-assertively

To react *non-assertively* is to appear passive, but the intrapersonal experience is quite different. Reacting *non-assertively* means that you are experiencing conflict at the intrapersonal level; you are bothered, upset, uncomfortable with the given situation, but you choose not to show any reaction to it.

In the situation above, a person might be quite upset by the fact that someone cut in front of them in a line, but a nonassertive reaction would be to keep that reaction inside and not show it. It is clear that reacting *non-assertively* does not resolve a conflict but simply contains it at the intrapersonal level. Such reactions often lead to increased levels of discomfort and tension, the result of which may manifest itself in hypertension and physical discomfort and disease.

Nonassertive behavior is characterized by an inability or unwillingness to communicate one's true feelings or ideas to others. This person disregards his or her own rights. This person would also like to win but may have a greater fear of losing and, therefore, is unwilling to compete. Another reason that many people choose to be nonassertive is so they will not appear aggressive.

Aggressively

Reacting *aggressively* is to outwardly express your discomfort in a direct, hostile, emotional, and often threatening manner. This reaction is typically confrontational and comes from a desire to "win," perhaps at any cost. It is directed *at* the other person or persons, and is typified by "you" messages that aim at laying blame and forcing capitulation. This kind of reaction may often leave the respondent feeling better, at least temporarily, but seldom resolves the conflict, since the other person placed in the "loser" role that often results in a desire to pay back or get even.

For example, reacting to a person who cut in line in front of you by yelling or them or by physically threatening them if they do not move would be reacting *aggressively.* Aggressive reactions may also prompt aggressive responses from the other person or persons. In the North American culture, it is frequent that males react more aggressively when confronted with a conflict, especially with other males.

Passive-aggressively

"Pay back" is the defining characteristic of reacting *passive-aggressively.* The behavior is highly manipulative, and often involves sarcasm. The outward sign of a passive-aggressive reaction is one of "passiveness." This is very similar to both "passive" and "non-assertive" reactions. The difference is what's going on inside of us. Internally, there is discomfort with the conflict situation but, as with nonassertiveness, a desire not to engage the other person directly regarding the conflict. The desire in reacting *passive-aggressively* is to get back at the other person, to act in a manner that will "teach them a lesson." The goal is to punish, or to win at all costs. A key to this type of reaction is that the other person "gets the message," that they are able to "connect the dots" between the reaction they see and the action that motivated it.

For example, reacting to someone cutting in line in front of you by loudly telling the person you're with how rude you think it is when someone cuts in the line or by racing ahead of them and cutting in front of them at the door would be reacting *passive-aggressively.* The goal is that the other person will "read their mind." The major problem here is that, often, the recipient can't or won't "connect the dots" and consequently the passive-aggressive reaction seems bizarre and without cause. In the North American culture, because of role training and expectations, females more frequently react *passive-aggressively.*

Assertively

Assertive behavior is defined as communicating in a direct, calm, honest, nonmanipulative manner, with respect for the rights of self and the other. Assertive persons are likely to see their world from a position of win-win. They take the position that each person can probably be satisfied if they openly communicate about what they need, why they need it, and what they will give up to get it. Through open and honest communication, they seek to understand the other and to be understood.

Many people have difficulty behaving in an assertive fashion because our society has not encouraged people to speak up for what they want while recognizing that others also have the right to do so. Reacting *assertively* requires speaking for yourself. Here, "I" messages replace the "you" messages of aggressive behavior. The goal is to speak for yourself while encouraging the other person to do the same.

Thinking, Behaving, and Speaking Assertively.

We will now examine ways to ask for what we want. Speaking up for what we want, respecting ourselves and others, and talking about what bothers us will help us to manage conflicts.

Your Rights (and Mine)

To begin with, assertion training is based on the assumption that all human beings have certain rights. It may be interesting to note that these "rights" have been based on the United Nation's "Bill of Human Rights," and have been modified over time to the list below:

1. I have the right to assert myself as a worthy individual.

2. I have the right to express myself.

3. I have the right to be listened to.

4. I have the right to change my mind.

5. I have the right to express my feelings without always justifying them.

6. I have the right to not always need the goodness of others to survive.

7. I have the right to say, "I don't know."

8. I have the right to say, "I don't understand."

9. I have the right to decide whether I want to be responsible for the problems of someone else.

10. I have the right to make mistakes and to accept responsibility for my actions.

11. I have the right, as an assertive person, to decide when and if I want to react assertively.

One note of caution before proceeding to our next main area: Assertion training can lead to too much "I-am-number-one." Many books and seminars written and presented under the guise of teaching people how to be assertive are really just teaching people how to get their way—all the time—no matter what. Always remember as you communicate with someone else that just as you have "rights," the other person has those same "rights."

Techniques and Strategies

In terms of possible techniques or verbal strategies, there are various approaches that can be used. The model widely used in this field comes from M. Smith's *When I Say No, I Feel Guilty,* in which the author presents seven basic techniques. For each technique, we will give a brief explanation and then present a sample situation and dialogue to illustrate their use.

Broken Record

Repeat your goal/request over and over without getting distracted and until you wear the other person down.

Situation: You have just received your credit card bill and find charges for purchases you never made—you (Y) contact customer service (S).

Y: You have my transaction on your screen? You see the $39.95 charge for shoes from Shu-World? I never shop at that store and I would like my account credited for that amount, please.

S: Well, we have the receipt and your signature is on it.

Y: You may have something that looks like my signature, but I never shop at that store and I would like my account credited for that amount, please.

S: It is highly unlikely that anyone would forge your signature for $39.95.

Y: I realize that you think it is highly unlikely, but I never shop at that store and I would like my account credited for that amount, please.

Fogging

Calmly and politely agreeing with your critic that there *may be* **some truth in what they are saying** or telling them that **you can understand why they** *might* **feel that way.** This buys time and puts you in control of the situation.

Situation: At the office, your boss (B) starts complaining that you (Y) are taking too many breaks and using the copier for personal use.

B: Not only do you take too many breaks but now you are using the company copier for your own personal use.

Y: Perhaps I should be more concerned about my break times and use of the copier.

Negative Assertion

Openly and honestly admitting your mistakes instead of hiding or lying about them. We all make mistakes.

Situation: At a friend's (F) party, you (Y) knock over a glass, which breaks.

F: That ruins my set, which has a lot of sentimental value.
Y: I feel very bad that I broke the glass and I wish I would not have.

Negative Inquiry

Asking for more criticism of yourself in order to get rid of criticism that is manipulative. It makes people tell you the truth about why they are angry.

Situation: You (Y) have decided to go away to college and now your closest friend (F) is criticizing your decision.

F: Why did you choose that diploma factory to go to? You won't learn anything there.
Y: I like the school. I don't know why you're so against my going there.
F: I can't believe you don't want to go to a good school.
Y: This is a good school and I still don't understand what you have against my going there.
F: But the students are all rejects from other colleges.
Y: I like this school. I know some of the students who go there and they like it. Are you sure there isn't some other reason you don't want me going to this school?

Free Information

This is a listening skill. You learn to ask lots of questions about others and their concerns, opinions, etc., rather than talking about yourself too much.

Situation: You (Y) have just started a new job and during lunch break meet another person (P), who mentions that they have just gotten back from vacation.

Y: That sounds great. What did you do during your time off?

Self-Disclosure

Admitting openly and honestly your strengths, weaknesses, and opinions without apologizing for them.

Situation: Your boss (B) asks you (Y) to do something that you do not know enough about.

B: When you've finished that report, take this software and make the spreadsheet and a graph of it.

Y: I know how to make the spreadsheet, but I'm not sure about the graph.

Workable Compromise

This is for two assertive people. For example, when you are both using broken record, you must compromise. This compromise does not have to be **fair**—it only has to **work**. Never use it if you feel that your self-respect will be jeopardized.

Situation: Your boss (B) needs a report by 10 a.m. the next day and asks you (Y) to stay late to finish it.

B: I need you to stay late and finish this report tonight. It must be done for an important meeting I have tomorrow at 10 a.m.

Y: I know this report is important to you, but I have a very important meeting after work.

B: But I **want** this report finished tonight.

Y: O.K. I will stay an extra hour today and if I don't finish, I will come in early tomorrow so that you have it for your 10 o'clock meeting.

How Assertive Are You?

PURPOSE

To help you assess your level of assertiveness.

PROCEDURE

1. Place an "X" on the following scale, indicating generally how assertive you believe yourself to be.

| nonassertive | 60 | 120 | 180 | 240 | 300 | completely assertive |

2. For each of the statements below, circle the number that best describes you. If an item describes a situation unfamiliar to you, try to imagine what your response would be. Of course, you will not achieve an accurate self-evaluation unless you answer all questions honestly.

Rating Scale

1 Never
2 Rarely
3 Sometimes
4 Usually
5 Always

1. I do my own thinking.	1	2	3	4	5
2. I can be myself around wealthy, educated, or prestigious people.	1	2	3	4	5
3. I am poised and confident among strangers.	1	2	3	4	5
4. I freely express my emotions.	1	2	3	4	5
5. I am friendly and considerate toward others.	1	2	3	4	5
6. I accept compliments and gifts without embarrassment or a sense of obligation.	1	2	3	4	5
7. I freely express my admiration of others' ideas and achievements.	1	2	3	4	5

8. I readily admit my mistakes.	1	2	3	4	5
9. I accept responsibility for my life.	1	2	3	4	5
10. I make my own decisions and accept the consequences.	1	2	3	4	5
11. I take the initiative in personal contacts.	1	2	3	4	5
12. When I have done something well, I tell others.	1	2	3	4	5
13. I am confident when going for job interviews.	1	2	3	4	5
14. When I need help, I ask others to help me.	1	2	3	4	5
15. When at fault, I apologize.	1	2	3	4	5
16. When I like someone very much, I tell them so.	1	2	3	4	5
17. When confused, I ask for clarification.	1	2	3	4	5
18. When someone is annoying me, I ask that person to stop.	1	2	3	4	5
19. When -someone cuts in front of me in line, I protest.	1	2	3	4	5
20. When treated unfairly, I object.	1	2	3	4	5
21. If I were underpaid, I would ask for a salary increase.	1	2	3	4	5
22. When I am lonely or depressed, I take action to improve my mental outlook.	1	2	3	4	5
23. When working at a job or task I dislike intensely, I look for ways to improve my situation.	1	2	3	4	5
24. I complain to the management when I have been overcharged or have received poor service.	1	2	3	4	5
25. When something in my house or apartment malfunctions, I see that the landlady repairs it.	1	2	3	4	5
26. When I am disturbed by someone smoking, I say so.	1	2	3	4	5

27. When a friend betrays my confidence, I tell that
person how I feel.   1   2   3   4   5

28. I ask my doctor all of the questions for which I
want answers.   1   2   3   4   5

29. I ask for directions when I need help finding my way.   1   2   3   4   5

30. When there are problems, I maintain a relationship
rather than cutting it off.   1   2   3   4   5

31. I communicate my belief that everyone at home should
help with the upkeep rather than doing it all myself.   1   2   3   4   5

32. I make sexual advances toward my husband or sex
partner.   1   2   3   4   5

33. When served food at a restaurant that is not prepared
the way I ordered it, I express myself.   1   2   3   4   5

34. Even though a clerk goes to a great deal of trouble
to show merchandise to me, I am able to say "No."   1   2   3   4   5

35. When I discover that I have purchased defective
merchandise, I return it to the store.   1   2   3   4   5

36. When people talk in a theater, lecture, or concert, I
am able to ask them to be quiet.   1   2   3   4   5

37. I maintain good eye contact in conversations.   1   2   3   4   5

38. I would sit in the front of a large group if the only
remaining seats were located there.   1   2   3   4   5

39. I would speak to my neighbors if their dog was
keeping me awake with its barking at night.   1   2   3   4   5

40. When interrupted, I comment on the interruption
and then finish what I am saying.   1   2   3   4   5

41. When a friend or spouse makes plans for me without
my knowledge or consent, I object.   1   2   3   4   5

42. When I miss someone, I express the fact that I want
to spend more time with that person.   1   2   3   4   5

43. When a person asks me to lend something and I really donot want to, I refuse.

   1   2   3   4   5

44. When a friend invites me to join her and I really don't want to, I turn down the request.

   1   2   3   4   5

45. When friends phone and talk too long on the phone, I can terminate the conversation effectively.

   1   2   3   4   5

46. When someone criticizes me, I listen to the criticism without being defensive.

   1   2   3   4   5

47. When people are discussing a subject and I disagree with their points of view, I express my difference of opinion.

   1   2   3   4   5

48. When someone makes demands on me that I don't wishto fulfill, I resist the demands.

   1   2   3   4   5

49. I speak up readily in group situations.

   1   2   3   4   5

50. I tell my children or family members the things I like about them.

   1   2   3   4   5

51. When my family or friends make endless demands on my time and energy, I establish firm notions about the amount of time I am willing to give.

   1   2   3   4   5

52. When my husband phones to tell me he is bringing home an unexpected guest for dinner and I've had a hard day at work, I level with him about it and request that he make alternative plans.

   1   2   3   4   5

53. When one friend is not meeting all of my needs, I establish meaningful ties with other people.

   1   2   3   4   5

54. When my own parents, in-laws, or friends freely give advice, I express appreciation for their concern without feeling obligated to follow their advice or suggestions.

   1   2   3   4   5

55. When someone completes a task or job for me with which I am dissatisfied, I ask that it be done correctly.

   1   2   3   4   5

56. When I object to political practices, I take actionr rathe than blaming politicians.

   1   2   3   4   5

57. When I am jealous, I explore the reasons for my feelings, and look for ways to increase my self-confidence and self-esteem.   1   2   3   4   5

58. When a person tells me she envies me, I accept her comments without feeling guilty or apologizing.   1   2   3   4   5

59. When I am feeling insecure, I assess my personal strengths and take action designed to make me feel more secure.   1   2   3   4   5

60. I accept my husband's, wife's, or boy/girl friend's interests in other people without feeling I must compete with them.   1   2   3   4   5

Total Score   _____

DISCUSSION

1. How does your initial general rating compare to your actual score? If there is a significant difference, how can you account for it?
2. How important is it to you to be a more assertive person? Why?
3. In what ways can you go about being more assertive?

"Empowering" Your Language

PURPOSE

To acknowledge and demonstrate responsibility for one's own ideas, statements, and behaviors, and by so doing, free ourselves to do what *we* decide to do.

PROCEDURE

For each of the words/phrases in the left column, substitute the words/phrases in the right column *for a period of one week.* During this time period, inform those with whom you communicate that you are changing your communication behavior as an experiment in determining how language affects thinking and behavior. Following the week-long experiment, *answer the following questions:*

1. What were your reactions to the changes? How did it feel? How did your behavior change?

2. What were others' reactions to the change? Did they react to you differently? If so, how?

3. Are you going to stick with the "empowering" words or go back to the "old ones" and why?

Replace	**With**
A. Got to / have to / must / should	I want / I will / I'm going to

Why: There are few things in life that we *have* to do; most things are a result of decisions that we make and by acknowledging this, we remind ourselves that we can decide to do things differently.

B. Can't	I won't / I don't want to / I will / I can

Why: There are very few things in life that are beyond our physical capability. By using "can't" we turn over control of our behavior to someone/something else. It is far easier to change a *won't* to a *will* than a *can't* to a *can.*

	Replace	**With**

C. Must have / need   I want

Why: Very few things are "musts" or "needs." Instead, they are the result of *our desires* and *wants*.

D. One / we / you / they   I / my / me

Why: Instead of "objectifying" our ideas and statements, we can acknowledge *responsibility* for our own ideas, thoughts, and feelings.

E. Every / all / none / never / always   Some / many / most / a few

Why: To remind ourselves that we can only speak for *our own limited experiences* and not overgeneralize in order to make our views seem greater.

F. Try   I am / I am not / I will / I won't

Why: Success in life is not determined by how hard we *try* to do something, but rather whether or not we *do it. Try* is an effort-oriented verb; *will* or *won't* are results-oriented, and acknowledge our responsibility for the results. A positive attitude can make miracles.

Five Sample Situations

PURPOSE

To be able to identify responses as either assertive, nonassertive, passive-aggressive or aggressive.

PROCEDURE

Read though each of the following situations and determine which of the four responses is assertive, which is nonassertive, which is passive-aggressive and which is aggressive.

1. Cousin Jessie, with whom you prefer not to spend much time, is on the phone. She says she is planning to spend the next three weeks with you.

   Responses:
   a. "We'd love to have you come and stay as long as you like."
   b. "We'd be glad to have you come for the weekend, but we cannot invite you for longer. A short visit will be very nice for all of us, and we'll want to see each other again."
   c. "The weather back here has been terrible (not true) so you'd better plan on going elsewhere."
   d. "So, will this be your usual six month visit?"

2. You have bought a toaster at Sears that doesn't work properly.

   Responses:
   a. Do you like hassling customers from your minimum wage job?
   b. "What right do you have selling me junk like this?"
   c. You put it in the closet and buy another one.
   d. "I bought this toaster and it doesn't work and I would like my money back."

3. One of your workers has been coming in late consistently for the last three or four days.

   Responses:
   a. "I have noticed that for the last few days you have been a little late and I am concerned about it."
   b. "It's nice of you to take time out of your busy day to drop by."
   c. You mumble to yourself and hope he'll be on time tomorrow.
   d. "The next time you're late, you're fired."

4. You are in a meeting and someone starts smoking, which offends you.

    Responses:
    a. "Hey, man, that smoke is terrible."
    b. You suffer the smoke in silence.
    c. "There's nothing I like better than the fresh smell of smoke in my air."
    d. "I would appreciate it if you wouldn't smoke here. I am bothered by it."

5. You are at a lecture with 400 other people. The speaker is not speaking loud enough for all to hear.

    Responses:
    a. Turning to the person next to you, you say, "It's so nice to pay this kind of money to hear a speaker talk to himself."
    b. You yell out, "Speak up; we can't hear you, idiot!"
    c. You raise your hand and get her attention—"Would you mind speaking a little louder, please."
    d. You continue straining to hear and end up daydreaming.

DISCUSSION

1. Was it easy or difficult to distinguish among the four behaviors?
2. Which of the situations were easier to distinguish, and why?

Assertion Training: Practicing Behaviors

PURPOSE

To be able to construct assertive, nonassertive and aggressive comments in different situations.

PROCEDURE

1. Form small groups.
2. As a group, take each of the 10 situations and write an assertive response for each.

1. You are in charge of a meeting and Jean walks in somewhat intoxicated.
2. You are talking with some other people and they start talking about Jose. Someone calls him a "wetback," which offends you, because Jose is your friend.
3. You are taking an English class. Your handwriting is the "pits." As a result, your teacher keeps giving you a lower grade, which you feel is unfair.
4. You and a group of friends have decided to go out to dinner. Everyone else wants to go somewhere that you do not like.
5. You want to go out for the weekend with a group of friends. Your parents object. You still want to go.
6. Someone moves into the apartment next to you and you would like to meet them.
7. You are standing in the check-out line at Super Market. Someone keeps pushing their cart into your back.
8. You and a friend are shopping. You see him stealing something, which you feel is wrong.
9. You are wearing a new outfit and someone compliments you on it.
10. Your friend has said she will meet you for lunch at 12:30. She arrives at 1:15—with no apologies—and you are irritated!

DISCUSSION

1. Did you find it easier to come up with nonassertive and aggressive comments than with assertive ones? Why?
2. Did you find it harder to come up with assertive comments to some situations as opposed to others? If so, which ones? Why?

Managing Conflict through Assertiveness

PURPOSE

To apply assertiveness principles to the management of conflicts.

PROCEDURE

1. Working on your own, complete the steps below.
2. After you have completed the steps, role-play the situation with a partner.

Step 1. Define the conflict that you are having with another person and the other person's shared responsibility in that conflict.

Step 2. Make an appointment with the other person. (Be sure to allow yourselves enough time to work through steps 3 through 6.)

Step 3. Describe the problem and your needs to the other person. (Describe the behavior, your interpretations, your feelings, and the consequences to you.)

Step 4. Seek to understand your partner. (Ask your partner to paraphrase what you said. Ask your partner to share what he or she wants from you. Be sure to paraphrase or do perception-checking on what you hear.)

Step 5. Use the *Workable Compromise* described in this chapter. (Remember, the key to workable compromise is that each party feels that it will work for them.)

Step 6. Put the solution into effect and plan a follow-up appointment to evaluate the extent to which your solution is working for each of you.

DISCUSSION

1. Which step(s) did you find the most difficult?
2. What changes in your own behavior will you need to focus on?

REACTIONS TO CHAPTER 8

1. Write your personal definition of conflict.

2. Describe your own comfort level in conflict situations.

3. Would you classify yourself as basically nonassertive, assertive, or aggressive?

4. In what kinds of situations do you find it most difficult to be assertive?

5. Describe a situation where it might be better to react aggressively.

6. Describe a situation where it might be better to be nonassertive.

7. Which simple concept from this chapter do you plan to apply first in your next conflict? How?

Relational Communication

We share a large part of our lives with other individuals in what we call "relationships." All relationships involve elements of interpersonal communication; however, the study of relational communication focuses specifically on the communicating that occurs between two people who are in the process of beginning, continuing, or ending a relationship with each other. Although we have many relationships (i.e., with neighbors, our boss, teachers), this chapter will address the intimate communication between family members, close friends, or significant love relationships. In order to gain an understanding of the communication process that occurs in these relationships, we will define several terms that will be used in this chapter:

◇ Relationships

Definition: The context in which continuing social interaction occurs.

Example: Whenever we communicate with anyone in an ongoing way, we, do that within a relational framework.

◇ Relational Communication

Definition: Communication that affects our willingness, and that of others, to initiate, continue, or terminate our relationships.

Examples: Greeting people, handshakes (initiating), expressing our commitment to the relationship (continuing), telling someone we no longer want to be friends (terminating), and so on.

◇ Relational Identity

Definition: The perception of two individuals in a relationship as something different from who they are as individuals.

Examples: We may see ourselves as a "couple," "twosome," or a "duo." We begin to refer to ourselves as "we" or "us" instead of "you and me."

◆ Intimacy

Definition: According to Adler, Rosenfeld, and Towne in their book *Interplay,* this can be classified in three areas: intellectual, emotional, and physical intimacy. Intimacy is characterized by extended and concentrated communication in any of these areas. It is also not the goal in all relationships.

Examples: We may share our life philosophies with a friend (intellectual), our feelings of love with a parent (emotional), and a sexual relationship with a girl friend or boy friend (physical).

◆ Self-Disclosure

Definition: Sharing information about oneself that the other individual is unlikely to find out by other means.

Examples: Sharing secrets, discoveries, confidential information, past history, and experiences or information that we do not commonly express.

THE IMPORTANCE OF RELATIONAL COMMUNICATION

Imagine for a moment that you are suddenly alone in the world. You woke up this morning and found that the people you share your home with are gone. You stepped outside and your neighborhood was void of the sounds of people awakening and preparing for a new day—no car engines running or doors closing as other individuals go about their daily routines. You leave for work or school only to find the streets empty. Every store, school, or business you see is the same: deserted. As far as you know, you are the only person left in the world!

This is not a very pleasant scene but it does allow us to examine how we feel about those who share our lives. Whether it be a parent, a roommate, or a spouse, we would sorely miss the company of others if we suddenly found them absent from our lives. The reality is that we are social creatures by nature and our relationships provide the foundation of our daily lives. Understanding how and why we establish these relationships, and what barriers we face in successfully maintaining them, can help us avoid the "disappearance" of important relationships from our lives. And, most importantly, the more we understand about how we communicate in these relationships, the greater the opportunity we have to make them work well.

Relationships Are Inevitable

Relationships are, fortunately, unavoidable. From business contacts to friendship to intimate love, relationships pervade our lives. We begin by being born into families where we learn the basics of communication in relationships.

Babies learn, through nonverbal communication with their parents, that certain people are more important to their experience than others. Toddlers discover that developing more relationships makes life more interesting. Brothers, sisters, grandparents, and others provide social opportunities and stimulation.

Relationships also fulfill basic human needs. Simply communicating with others is not enough. We need to know that significant people share a future with us. We need companionship, love, and a sense of belonging. And we don't fulfill these needs in any one relationship. Instead, we often have several or many relationships that serve us differently. We may socialize with one friend and confide in another. And we fulfill others' needs as well. This is the reciprocal nature of relationships. As long as we are both having our needs met we can be quite satisfied with each other. However, as soon as one person starts to expect more than the other person is willing to give, or if one person feels she is giving more than she is receiving, then we have a "needs" imbalance and the relationship may suffer as a consequence.

Relationships Develop in Stages

Effective relationships need to be carefully created and constructively maintained. The path a relationship takes does not happen by accident; we can exercise some degree of control by understanding how communication influences the development of relationships. According to researcher Mark Knapp in the book *Interpersonal Communication and Human Relationships,* relationships develop through the following 10 stages:

- Initiating. In this stage we want to create the impression that we are an interesting person worth knowing. At the same time we are evaluating the other individual's reaction to us. Initiating is often characterized by communication such as a handshake or "nice to meet you." If we are really interested in initiating a relationship, we often strategically plan our approach. Being "accidentally" in the same place at the same time, smiling, or nodding may gain us the entrance we desire.

- Experimenting. At this point we try to find things that we have in common with the other person. We often engage in "small talk." Now, you may be one of those people who find small talk to be superficial and useless, but at this early stage of a relationship it serves an important communication function. Besides finding out if we have anything in common, it helps us determine if we want to pursue the next step.

  For instance, Anthony had wanted to meet Brenda for a long time. When he finally got the courage to introduce himself, he suddenly started telling his life story, including some intimate details. When he asked her out to dinner, she turned him down. Little did he know that she was very uncomfortable with what he had told her. Brenda felt that Anthony was either insecure or moving "too fast!" Small talk would have broken the ice for Anthony and allowed the relationship to develop along a more natural path.

- Intensifying. At this point we begin to develop a relationship that will, hopefully, meet our needs. This stage is characterized by informal communication.

We start referring to each other as "we" rather than "I" or "you." We begin disclosing more about ourselves as the potential for growth becomes obvious. It is here that we find the courage to start expressing our feelings about commitment. Sheri, a college student, stated in class, "I have a friendship that has become very important to me. Yesterday my friend told me that we're going to be friends forever! I can't tell you how nice it is to know I can count on her."

- Integrating. In this stage a relational identity is developed. We are recognized by others as a "couple," "partners," or "buddies." We begin interacting with each other based on this new identity called "us." For example, Matthew canceled an appointment so he could go to his girl friend's company picnic with her. When we integrate, we often make rational commitments rather than continue to follow our individual schedules.

- Bonding. Now we make our commitment known through public rituals. A wedding is an example of such a ritual. Research in psychology indicates that public commitments create in us a stronger desire to make the relationship work. We decide to let the "world" know that we are having a relationship.

- Differentiating. We reach a point where the relational identity may be too restricting and we want to re-establish our own identities. Often this is a reaction to conflict in the relationship. For instance, a wife may stop referring to the family automobile as "our car" and start calling it "my car" in an effort to communicate her individuality. This doesn't mean that differentiation cannot have a positive outcome. Recognizing the other person's need for individuality and personal space can strengthen the original commitment to each other.

- Circumscribing. Hopefully all relationships will have happy endings, but we all know this is not realistic. At some point what we have with another person begins to deteriorate. The first stage of this disintegration is circumscribing, wherein we reduce the quantity or quality of time and energy we put into the relationship. For example, Tony and Sophie became a clear case of a relationship in this stage when they both started spending more time with other friends, avoiding each other's phone calls, and responding to each other by saying "you wouldn't be interested" or "it doesn't concern you." The sad part is that, while avoiding each other, we often avoid the fact that we are both contributing to the disintegration of what we called us.

- Stagnation. Here we really begin to live life in a rut! The relationship has no novelty or excitement and we react to it in a very routine way. Have you ever had a job that you disliked but you continued to perform? It becomes robotic, repetitive, and boring. The same thing happens to a relationship if we allow it to stagnate. We become the stereotypical picture of the old couple living in the same house and never speaking a word to each other.

- Avoiding. Stagnation may develop to the point that we cannot handle any contact with each other, so we go out of our way to avoid one another. For example, Angela, who dated Mario for two months, wanted so badly to avoid him that she dropped out of two classes that they attended together. Avoiding is a clear sign of the death of the relational identity. We no longer talk about "us"; rather we communicate in terms "you" or "me."

- Terminating. This is, of course, when one or both parties involved end the relationship can be brought on by the death of one of the individuals or a decision that staying together is no longer beneficial. This is one of the most difficult stages, for it can often be painful to the parties involved. How it occurs often depends on how intimate the relationship was. A casual friendship may end, but a marriage or cutting the ties with a family member may take more negotiation and expressing of feelings.

Most communication researchers agree that all relationships follow a systematic development. However, that doesn't mean that every time we get involved with someone it is destined for termination. What is important is that we discover how to stop the pattern when we've reached a stage where both participants are happy, and maintain the relationship at that level.

Overcoming Barriers to Developing Relationships

Initiating Relationships

There are many barriers to maintaining good communication in a relationship. However, the first major barrier is how to begin a relationship, how to initiate contact. We have probably all experienced the desire to meet someone and the uncertainty about how to go about communicating with them. Regardless of the kind of relationship we're interested in establishing (we may want a new friend or a new love), we face the barriers of overcoming our own shyness, having our advances rejected, and taking the risk of putting ourselves on the line. But if a relationship is going to exist, someone has to make the first move.

Arthur Wassmer, in his book *Making Contact,* recommends the SOFTENS Techniques to help-make the initial contact more productive. He uses each letter of the word "softens" to represent nonverbal behaviors that we can use when breaking the ice with someone new. Taking these nonverbal signals into consideration can help us overcome the fear we often feel on the initial contact. The technique is as follows:

- Smiling—genuinely done, helps establish a positive climate

- Open posture—communicates interest

- Forward lean—communicates involvement

- Touching by shaking hands—establishes physical contact

- Eye contact—communicates interest and listening, and builds rapport

- Nodding—communicates listening and can help you focus on what the other person is saying

- Space—can promote closeness depending on culture and the kind of relationship you want to encourage

The second barrier we face is communicating within the relationship in such a manner that we maintain the relationship. The more intimate the relationship is, the more complex it may become to maintain, whether it is with a family member, a friend, or a lover. Intimacy, whether physical, emotional, or intellectual, can enhance the relationship by allowing two people to bond to each other through this closeness, or it can drive them a-part if-one or the other is not ready or prepared to maturely deal with the intimacy.

Intimacy involves vulnerability and therefore requires trust in each other. If we feel like we are being manipulated or played with, we often find it difficult to be intimate with someone. This can happen when we encounter "control factors." Control factors are any issues in a relationship that cause one or more participants to feel a lack of balance in the relationship. In other words, these factors set things out of control. Several major communication control factors that surface in many relationships are:

- Unequal participation. Teresa feels she puts out a lot more effort in the marriage than her husband, Chris. She is feeling very dissatisfied with this imbalance and wants him to contribute his share to the relationship.

- Simultaneous Relationships. Rod and Mike have been friends for a long time. Recently, Mike became involved in a club at school and has been spending a lot less time with Rod. Rod, who has no interest in the club's activities, has made a request for more of Mike's time. Mike feels a tremendous imbalance. He wants to see Rod, but also continue developing his new relationships. He feels like he's doing a juggling act with friends.

- Incompatibility. Jennifer and Troy are very attracted to each other. They feel there is a real chemistry between them. However, as they start to spend time together, they find they have little in common. They want to see each other because of the interpersonal attraction, but when together, they have a tendency to argue over opposing viewpoints. They want to resolve this imbalance but don't know how.

- Game Playing. Matt feels confused about his relationship with his father. They can be getting along one day, but the next day his father is putting "some guilt trip on me." He would like to spend more time at home but the emotional "yo-yo" is getting to be more than he can handle.

- Control. Jesse is realizing that she is tired of being considered a "little girl" by her parents. Granted, they controlled her life when she was small, but she wants to make her own decisions now. She does not want the scales to lean go heavily in her parents' favor.

In each of these situations, the individuals involved feel an imbalance in their relationships. Each one has a choice: they can continue to feel the lack of satisfaction, they can reduce the amount of involvement in the relationship, or they can try to resolve the conflict by communicating with their partners about the factor causing the problem. The last option is necessary if the relationships are going to be maintained at a positive stage. But this step also requires willingness to self-disclose feelings in an honest and supportive fashion. If they are willing to take the risk of disclosure, then they have the chance to bring balance back to the relationship.

But disclosure must be given in appropriate amounts. We can overwhelm another person with our inner feelings and literally chase them away. If handled sensitively, self-disclosure has two benefits for relationships: it encourages reciprocal disclosure (I will be more motivated to share if you are equally willing), and it can increase the intimacy of the relationship.

Lastly, it is important to be aware of the influence self-disclosure has in our lives. It is not only important in maintaining healthy relationships, but it is also one of the first things to diminish as the relationship begins to deteriorate. Relationships that are stagnating are often characterized by a lack of disclosure—the individuals just won't share!

Ending a Relationship

The last barrier we'll address here deals with ending a relationship. For most of us this is one of the most difficult communication situations. Few of us want to play the "bad guy." Yet, if our partner is the one ending the relationship, we may suffer feelings of rejection and a loss of self-esteem. It is very rare to have an outcome where both parties are happy; however, this can happen. For example, Raul was tired of his girl friend, Janie, playing games; Janie was fed up with Raul continually trying to control her time. So they mutually agreed to call it quits and both were happy.

Most of us, however, suffer a feeling of loss when we lose relationships, whether they be through the death of a family member or the breakup of a love relationship. We are literally in mourning for the relational identity, that element that was composed of ourselves and another. We not only miss the other person but we miss that identity that was "us." As in any mourning situation, acknowledging our grief and allowing it to run its course is one of the best treatments to the pain of an ended relationship.

Knowing why we need relationships in our lives helps us understand the way we communicate within them. We are striving to start and maintain them, but sometimes find ourselves in one that is ending. Relationships, like life, work in a cycle. And, like life, how much we gain from them. The activities in this Chapter are designed to help you determine the kind of relationships you want and how to improve the ones you are currently involved in, and aid you in acquiring the skills to start new ones. With this information you will, hopefully, never find yourself alone in the world.

Relationship Expectations Activity

PURPOSE

To enable you to explore the expectations that males and females have for relationships with one another.

PROCEDURE

1. Divide into same-sex small groups.
2. Each group should make a list of the expectations that they have for a relationship with the opposite sex.
3. Once this list is put together, the group should pick its top 5 expectations.
4. As a group, discuss what are you willing to do or give up to get these expectations met.
5. Next, each group should put together the list of expectations that they think the opposite sex has for them, and identify what they think will be the top 5 expectations that the opposite sex will have.

DISCUSSION

1. As a class, discuss each group's list of expectations, and what they would be willing to do or give up to achieve their expectations.
2. Compare your guesses about the opposite sex's expectations to the expectations identified by the opposite sex. How accurately did your group guess the expectations of the opposite sex?
3. How similar are the expectations that the two sexes have for one another?
4. How can all of these expectations affect initiating and maintaining a relationship?
5. With respect to expectations, what can you do to establish healthy and satisfactory relationships?

TALKING TO PEOPLE IN OUR LIVES

The following five activities are designed to teach you the communication skills of initiating, maintaining and ending a conversation. The activities may be done singly or in a series.

Skill #1: Figuring Out Who to Talk To

PURPOSE

To learn to identify nonverbal signals that tell us if a person is willing to have a conversation.

PROCEDURE

1. For three days observe people you do not know but to whom you are attracted (as a possible friend or love interest).
2. Identify nonverbal signals that communicate to you whether a person is approachable or not (state specifically what the person is doing that makes you feel this way).
3. Describe the communication behavior below.

Not Approachable	**Approachable**
1.	1.
2.	2.
3.	3.
4.	4.
5.	5.
6.	6.
7.	7.

DISCUSSION

1. What did the "approachable" people do that made you feel this way? The "unapproachable?"
2. Which person seemed to be the most approachable, and why?
3. Which person seemed to be the most unapproachable, and why?
4. How approachable do you think other people perceive you, and why?
5. How will these observations help you in your future relationships?

PURPOSE

To examine the value of small talk as a way to initiate communication in a new relationship.

PROCEDURE

1. Select someone you do not know very well and initiate a conversation on one of the following topics: the weather, your favorite foods or hobbies, your jobs, a TV program or movie you've recently seen, a current news event, or the surrounding environment.
2. Carry on the conversation for at least 15 minutes, changing subjects if necessary to maintain dialogue.

DISCUSSION

1. How comfortable/uncomfortable were you using small talk?
2. Did small talk help you find areas of common interest?
3. Did small talk lead to any in-depth conversation? Explain.
4. How can small talk help you start a relationship with someone you're interested in?
5. How can small talk be used in your current significant relationships?

Skill #3: Sharing Yourself— More In-Depth Conversations

PURPOSE

To explore the value of sharing personal information as a means of encouraging in-depth conversation.

PROCEDURE

1. Over the next week monitor the conversation you have with family members, friends, and significant love relationships. Select five occasions when you share personal information about yourself with one or more of these people.
2. If you do not normally share personal information, then select five opportunities to do so.
3. For each occasion, describe the following:
   a. My partner was:
   b. The information I shared was:
   c. His/her response was:

DISCUSSION

1. Did the personal information encourage more conversation? Why or why not?
2. How did the person respond? How did you feel about his/her response?
3. How can sharing personal information enhance your relationships?

PURPOSE

To explore the use of open-ended questions (questions that invite a variety of responses rather than a short, specific answer) as a means to maintain a conversation.

PROCEDURE

1. For each situation below, write two open-ended questions that could keep the conversation going.
2. Divide into dyads.
3. Ask each other the questions you have just written. Take turns role-playing and responding.

Situation 1: You are out on a blind date. You and your partner are sitting in a nice restaurant and are looking at the menus. The restaurant overlooks the ocean and it is sunset.

1.

2.

Situation 2: You are visiting a good friend's home for the first time and have just sat down for lunch. The friend's two young children are playing in the next room.

1.

2.

Situation 3: It's the first meeting of class. You sit down next to a person whom you have been attracted to for some time but haven't approached before now.

1.

2.

Situation 4: You've just met your fiance's/fiancee's parents for the first time. You are alone with them in their living room.

1.

2.

DISCUSSION

1. Was it difficult to come up with your questions and, if so, why?
2. Did the open-ended questions encourage conversation between you and your partner? Why or why not?
3. How might open-ended questions enhance communication in your relationships?

Skill #5: It's Hard to Stop Talking

PURPOSE

To experience the process of ending a conversation.

PROCEDURE

1. You will practice the following methods of ending a conversation:
   a. Summary—identifies the main points of the discussion: "I really understand how to organize this surprise party, Mom. I'll get started on the supplies right away."
   b. Value—a supportive statement that points out something that you found useful or are appreciative about: "This talk has helped so much! I really appreciate how much you've listened to my problem."
   c. Future Interest—identifies your desire to meet again: "I would really like to talk further with you about this. Could we get together later today?"
2. For each of the following situations, write an example of one of the three preceding methods of ending a conversation. Identify which one you are using:

Situation 1: Disagreement with a parent:

Situation 2: After listening to a close friend who talked about his troubled love life all evening:

Situation 3: After an unenjoyable dinner date:

Situation 4: After having a great date with someone you haven't seen in several years.

DISCUSSION

1. Do you normally find it difficult to end conversations? Explain.
2. Was it difficult to come up with these endings? Why or why not?
3. How can using specific endings help your communication in your relationships?

PURPOSE

This test is based upon a growing amount of research regarding gender differences in communication behaviors. The questions are intended to be general, and therefore do not address all situations or all people.

PROCEDURE

Mark a "T" If you think each of the following statements is true, and an "F" if you think it is false.

True or False

_____	1. Women's language is more direct than men's.
_____	2. Men seek assistance from others more than women.
_____	3. Women try to change others more than men.
_____	4. Men are more jealous than women.
_____	5. Women boast about their successes more than men.
_____	6. Women would rather be respected than loved.
_____	7. Men need more "space" (private time) than women.
_____	8. Women respond better to stress than men.
_____	9. Men seek approval from others more than women.
_____	10. Winning through intimidation is a male skill.
_____	11. Women are more decisive than men.
_____	12. Men like to give orders more than women.
_____	13. Women are more apologetic than men.
_____	14. Men tell more jokes and stories than women.
_____	15. Women usually dominate public discussions.
_____	16. Men accept words at face value more than women.
_____	17. Women take more physical risks than men.

True or False

	18.	Men talk about feelings more than women.
_____	19.	More women than men are worriers.
_____	20.	Men would rather talk about things than people.
_____	21.	Women avoid verbal confrontation more than men.
_____	22.	Men "nag" (repeat requests) more than women.
_____	23.	Women interrupt others more than men.
_____	24.	Men gossip about others as much as women.
_____	25.	Women want to be married more than men.
_____	26.	Men talk on the phone more than women.
_____	27.	Women are more facially animated than men.
_____	28.	Men's posture leans toward others more often than women's.
_____	29.	Men talk about health matters more than women.
_____	30.	Women have about one-tenth as much testosterone as men.

Scoring

28–30 correct	Excellent
25–27 correct	Good
21–24 correct	Fair
20 or fewer correct	Bewildered

DISCUSSION

1. How did you score on this test?
2. How can an inability to recognize the differences in behavior between women and men affect communication and relationships?
3. What surprises did you discover from this activity?

Pp 10–11 "How Well Do You Know Women and Men," excerpted from *He and She* (now *Opposite Sides of the Bed*) by Cris Evatt, with permission of Conari Press, an imprint of Red Wheel/Weiser, Boston, MA and York Beach, ME. To order call: 1-800-423-7087

ARE MEN AND WOMEN REALLY DIFFERENT?

Communication between the sexes has long been the brunt of jokes. Several popular sitcoms base episodes on family problems, with the fun being poked at the difference between the way the man and woman see things. It does make us laugh, until we find ourselves living the joke. What has created the stereotype that is so prevalent? The late Dr. Paul Popenoe, founder of the American Institute for Family Relations in Los Angeles, wrote a brief article in which he discussed the differences between men and women.

Beginning with the obvious, the functions of menstruation, pregnancy, and lactation, men and women are found to be fundamentally different. The depth and intensity of a woman's motherly feeling is associated with the length and flow of her menstrual period. She has different hormones from man, and the internal glandular secretions cause marked changes in her behavior, often related to emotional instability—she laughs and cries more easily.

A summary of studies over time, related by Dr. Katherine Dalton in *The Premenstrual Syndrome,* shows a large portion of crimes committed by females are clustered in the premenstrual period—along with suicides, accidents, a decline in the quality of school work, and declines in intelligence scores, visual acuity, and response speed.

Indeed, men and women are different in every cell of their bodies. The difference in the XY chromosome combination is the basic cause of development into maleness or femaleness. Perhaps because of this, a woman will outlive her male counterpart by three or four years in the United States.

These, together with the list that follows, are only some of the differences between men and women. Taking these differences into consideration makes it easier to understand why men and women have difficulty communicating. These differences should not become excuses for failing to communicate, but should be used to wake us to the need to work at communication.

Pain shared is halved. Joy shared is doubled.
—D. Corkille-Briggs

Man	Woman
Man normally has a higher basal metabolism. He is turning on the air conditioner when she is wrapped in a blanket.	Woman has a lower basal metabolism. She stands higher temperatures, and is cold more easily.
Man has a smaller stomach, kidneys, liver, and appendix, and larger lungs. In brute strength, men are 50% above women.	Women have a shorter head, broader face, chin less protruding, shorter legs, and longer trunk.
When the working day in British factories, under wartime conditions, was increased from 10 to 12 hours, accidents of men did not increase at all; women increased 150%.	Woman's blood contains more water (20% fewer red cells). Since these cells supply oxygen to the body cells, she tires more easily and is prone to faint.
Men's brains are specialized—the left side of the brain tends to handle verbal tasks and the right side handles spatial tasks.	The connecting tissue in a woman's brain is thicker, allowing for faster cross-over of information.
Men are attentive to things, and are more likely to be distracted by novel objects.	Women are better at perceiving subliminal messages and better at remembering details.
Men are more analytical—they think more abstractly. They have a knack for taking a situation out of context and analyzing it.	Women have a more complex thought process. They are more observant of the context around an experience. They can take in more information, on different levels.
Men seek closure in a group situation. They desire direct communication.	Women are comfortable with open-ended conversations and complexity.
Men have difficulties communicating sadness.	Women have a hard time expressing anger.
Men tend to interrupt more often, and speak longer.	Women tend to be better listeners.

PURPOSE

Understand how and why males and females communicate the way they do in relationships.

PROCEDURE

1. Divide into two large groups, one female and the other male.
2. Both groups will brainstorm questions that they always wanted to ask the opposite sex about some aspect of their communication behavior. **No "gender-bashing" is permitted.**
3. When the groups have finished brainstorming their lists, they should then pick their top 3 questions and give them to the instructor.
4. The groups should then sit facing each other; the instructor will select questions to ask each side.
5. Volunteers from the group being questioned can respond for their group.

Discussion

1. Did your group have difficulty coming up with questions? Why or not?
2. What differences/similarities did you notice about the kinds of issues the males and females were interested in?
3. Did you learn anything new about the way the opposite sex communicates in relationships? If so, what?
4. What, if any, changes can you make in your communication, given the answers you received from the opposite sex?
5. How would asking questions such as these in your significant relationships improve your understanding of those relationships and your communication?

Diagnosing Your Relationship

PURPOSE

To identify strengths and weaknesses of a specific relationship that you are in.

PROCEDURE

1. Select a relationship that is important to you (family, friend, or significant love relationship).
2. For each statement below, place an initial on each line as to how it relates to the relationship you have selected.
3. After completing all statements, review each one and analyze how satisfied you feel, using the rating scale.

Rating Scale

S   =   Satisfactory
OK =   Acceptable but not exceptional
D   =   Somewhat disappointing

You may have marked an item low on the continuum and like it that way. Or you may have marked an item high but feel uncomfortable about it. One person's intimacy is another's anxiety!

1. *Cooperation*
   A. We identify, define and solve our problems together. We respect each other's competence.
      Rarely . . . . .Often

   B. We work together as a team without competing or putting each other down.
      Rarely . . . . .Often

   C. We make decisions together. We make the most of what each of us has to contribute.
      Rarely . . . . .Often

   D. We share our opinions, thoughts, and ideas without becoming argumentative or defensive.
      Rarely . . . . .Often

   E. Overall, I am satisfied with our mutual respect and cooperation in thinking, deciding, and working together.
      Rarely . . . . .Often

Gerald L. Wilson, Alan M. Hantz and Michael S. Hanna, adapted from *Interpersonal Growth Through Communication*, 1989; William C. Brown Publishers.

2. *Compatibility*
   A.   We accept and work through our differences to find a common lifestyle
        with regard to our social and public images.
        Rarely . . . . .Often

   B.   We accept and work through our differences to find common values with
        regard to religion, morality, social concerns, and politics.
        Rarely . . . . .Often

   C.   We accept and work through our differences with regard to our social life
        and choice of friends.
        Rarely . . . . .Often

   D.   We accept and work through our differences so that we are able to share a
        basic approach to roles and rules.
        Rarely . . . . .Often

   E.   Overall, I am satisfied with the way we deal with our differences,
        maintain a lifestyle, and share values.
        Rarely . . . . .Often

3 *Intimacy*
   A.   We often play together. We put fun into what we do together.
        Rarely . . . . .Often

   B.   We express our emotions and feelings openly and freely. We say that we
        are scared, sad, hurting, angry, or happy.
        Rarely . . . . .Often

   C.   We tell each other what we like and dislike. We ask openly for what we
        want from each other.
        Rarely . . . . .Often

   D.   We "let go" with each other. We play, relax, and have fun with each other.
        Rarely . . . . .Often

   E.   Overall, I am satisfied with the level of openness and intimacy in our
        relationship.
        Rarely . . . . .Often

4. *Emotional Support*
   A.   We listen, understand, and empathize with each other's disappointments,
        hurts, or problems.
        Rarely . . . . .Often

   B.   We encourage and support each other when one of us is making basic life
        changes or trying new behavior.
        Rarely . . . . .Often

C. We take responsibility for nurturing when either of us is sick or hurting.
Rarely . . . . .Often

D. We are emotionally supportive of each other when either of us feels anxious, dependent, or in need of care.
Rarely . . . . .Often

E. Overall, I am satisfied with the nurturing and support we give to and receive from each other.
Rarely . . . . .Often

DISCUSSION

1. What relationship strengths were you able to identify from this analysis? What weaknesses?
2. What communication areas would you like to work on in this relationship?
3. Overall, how satisfied are you with the information you have discovered about this relationship, and why?
4. What have you learned from this analysis that can enhance other significant relationships in your life?

Self-Disclosure Questionnaire

PURPOSE

To discover how much of ourselves we disclose to other people.
To realize that different people affect what and how much we disclose of ourselves.

PROCEDURE

1. The answer sheet on the following pages has columns with the headings "Mother," "Father," "Sibling" (brother or sister), "Female Friend," "Male Friend," "Spouse," and "Significant Other."
2. You are to read each item on the questionnaire, then indicate on the answer sheet the extent that you have talked about each item to the person, that is, the extent to which you have made yourself known to that person. Use the rating scale provided.
3. Be sure to think of only one person in each category throughout the entire survey. Do not, for example, skip from one friend to another. Select one person for each category and then answer according to what you have talked about with the person.

ATTITUDES AND OPINIONS

1. What I think and feel about religion, my personal views.
2. My personal opinions and feelings about religious groups other than my own (e.g., Protestants, Catholics, Jews, atheists, etc.).
3. My views on the present government—the president, government, policies, etc.
4. My personal views on sexual morality—how I feel that I and others ought to behave in sexual matters.
5. My views on the question of racial integration in schools, transportation, etc.
6. My views on social movements (e.g., women's rights, gay liberation, ecology action, affirmative action, etc.).

TASTES AND INTERESTS

7. My favorite foods; the way I like food prepared and my food dislikes.
8. The kinds of movies that I like to see best, the TV shows that are my favorites.
9. The style of house, and the kinds of furnishings that I like best.
10. The kind of party or social gathering that I like best, and the kind that bore me or that I wouldn't enjoy.
11. My favorite ways of spending spare time (e.g., hunting, reading, cards, sports events, parties, dancing, etc.).
12. To what extent I use alcohol/drugs.

WORK (OR STUDIES)

13. What I find to be the worst pressures and strains in my work.
14. What I feel are my shortcomings and handicaps that prevent me from working as I'd like to, or that prevent me from getting further ahead in my work.
15. How I feel that my work is appreciated by others (e.g., boss, fellow workers, teacher, husband, etc.).
16. How I feel about the choice of career that I have made; whether I am satisfied with it.
17. How I really feel about the people I work for, or work with.
18. My own strengths and weaknesses as an employee.
19. Whether I owe money, if so, how much?
20. All of my present sources of income (e.g., wages, fees, allowances, etc.).
21. My total financial worth, including property, savings bonds, insurance, etc.
22. My most pressing need for money right now (e.g., outstanding bills, some major purchase that is desired or needed).
23. How I budget my money, the proportion that goes to necessities, etc.
24. To what extent money is important to me.

PERSONALITY

25. The aspects of my personality that I dislike, worry about, or regard as a handicap to me.
26. Things in the past or present that I feel ashamed or guilty about.
27. What it takes to get me really worried, anxious, and afraid.

28. What it takes to hurt my feelings deeply.
29. The kinds of things that make me especially proud of myself, elated, full of esteem and self-respect.
30. The things about my personality that I would really like to change.

BODY

31. How I wish I looked, my ideals for overall appearance.
32. Whether I have any long-range worries about health (e.g., cancer).
33. My present physical measurements (e.g., height, weight, waist, etc.).
34. My feelings about my adequacy in sexual behavior; whether I feel able to perform adequately in sex relationships.
35. Whether I have any health problems (e.g., allergies, headaches, heart condition, etc.).
36. The physical characteristics I admire about myself.

BEHAVIOR

37. What the various roles that I "act out" are.
38. The extent to which I like or dislike these roles.
39. Which role is most like me, and why.
40. The extent to which society's stereotyping influences my behavior and interaction with other people.
41. To what extent do I play "games" in order to be socially accepted.
42. To what extent does tactile communication (touching) play in my communication behavior.

COMMUNICATION

43. To what extent do I say what I am really thinking at the time.
44. To what extent do I use profanity for shock value.
45. To what extent do I use nonverbal communication for social gain (e.g., possessions, dress, appearance, cues, etc.).
46. My strengths relative to self-confidence in expressing my opinions.
47. The aspects of my communication I like (e.g., straightforward, clarity, organized, etc.).
48. Whether I am self-conscious about speaking in public, and why.

Self-Disclosure Rating Scale

3 I have talked in full and complete detail about this item to the other person. This person knows me fully in this respect, and could describe me accurately.

2 I have talked specifically to this person, yet have felt hesitant to talk in complete detail. This person knows me well, but not fully in this respect.

1 I have talked in general terms about this item. The other person has only a general idea about this aspect of me.

0 I have told the other person nothing about this aspect of me.

–3 I have lied or misrepresented myself to the other person about this aspect of me.

	Mother	Father	Sibling	Female Friend	Male Friend	Spouse	Significant Other
1							
2							
3							
4							
5							
6							
7							
8							
9							
10							
11							
12							
13							
14							
15							
16							
17							
18							
19							
20							
21							
22							
23							
24							
25							
26							
27							
28							

	Mother	Father	Sibling	Female Friend	Male Friend	Spouse	Significant Other
29							
30							
31							
32							
33							
34							
35							
36							
37							
38							
39							
40							
41							
42							
43							
44							
45							
46							
47							
48							
Totals							

DISCUSSION

1. To whom do you reveal yourself the most?
2. What is it about these relationships that causes you to reveal yourself?
3. To whom do you reveal yourself the least?
4. Do the roles that you and the other people assume in your daily lives affect your self-disclosure in your relationships with them?
5. What kinds of things do you reveal the most? The least?
6. Does the amount of self-disclosure with each person satisfy you, or should there be more self-disclosure with certain people and less self-disclosure with others?
7. Did the results of the questionnaire surprise you? If so, how/why?

Relationship Roles

PURPOSE

To examine the different purposes that different significant relationships serve in our lives.

PROCEDURE

1. For each situation below, list three people whom you would select to meet the situation.
2. List these people in the order of whom you would call on first, second, and third.
3. Explain why you picked each person.

Situation

You are stranded 200 miles from home and need someone to drive your brand new sports car to you. Whom would you ask?

Person	Reason
1.	
2.	
3.	

Situation

You are going out of town for two weeks and need someone to stay at your house and take care of your pets. Whom would you ask?

Person	Reason
1.	
2.	
3.	

Situation

You have been offered another job and feel very uncertain about taking it. With whom would you discuss this offer?

Person   **Reason**

1.

2.

3.

Situation

You just broke up with a person whom none of your friends or family likes very well. With whom would you share the news?

Person   **Reason**

1.

2.

3.

Situation

You have just been informed that you are the winner of the *Readers' Digest* Sweepstakes. Whom would you tell?

Person   **Reason**

1.

2.

3.

DISCUSSION

1. Was it difficult selecting people for any of the situations? Why or why not?
2. How does the situation change the way we communicate with others?
3. What did you learn about these relationships and the roles they play in your life?

CONNECTIONS

1. Smile! It makes your face light up and your eyes sparkle.

2. Say hello to strangers. It feels good to be acknowledged.

3. Look people in the eye when you are with them. Show them they are your present priority.

4. Remember and use people's names when you speak to them. It makes them feel valued.

5. Focus on the positive. Everyone has something to contribute that is useful.

6. Praise freely—but require a request for criticism.

7. Be tolerant. There are as many opinions and preferences as there are people.

8. Give freely to others. The best reward is knowing you have made a difference.

9. Be enthusiastic. Passion is contagious and magnetic.

10. Have patience. Have you ever had a bad day?

Name _____

Date _____

Your professor may require this exercise to be handed in.

REACTIONS TO CHAPTER 9

1. List three examples of relationships in your life where your communication has been influenced by the stage each relationship is in. Describe how communication is used in these relationships.

2. What kinds of barriers do you encounter that make it difficult to maintain important relationships?

3. How does self-disclosure influence your relationships?

4. How does understanding the role of communication in relationships help you establish and maintain meaningful relationships in your life?

Job Search Skills

A perfect time to apply your communication skills is during the job search process. For example, the networking process will afford you an opportunity to use both your verbal and nonverbal skills as you meet people who will give you information about their particular field and perhaps help you join them in that world. Clear and thoughtful writing in your cover letter and resume will attract attention of prospective employers who will invite you to an interview. Finally, the employment interview offers you the opportunity to manage both your verbal and nonverbal communication skills.

◈ Cover Letter

A letter adapted for a particular end that highlights one's background with specific items that most relate to the needs of a prospective employer. You tailor your experiences to the employer's anticipated needs.

◈ Resume

A selective, well-organized synopsis of your education, accomplishments, and special skills. The resume is a brief sales device designed to communicate your value as an employee.

◈ Networking

The art of making and using contacts who can help you reach your objective. You identify people who can supply you with important information and resources.

◈ Employment Interviewing

A highly concentrated face-to-face meeting designed to explore the interviewee's qualifications and determine a job "fit."

The Importance of Job Search Skills

The Bureau of Labor Statistics estimates that the average worker will have six employers in the course of a lifetime. The average worker searches for a job once every three to four years.

Generally, the harder you work at job hunting, the quicker you will find employment. Many people begin the job search process and fail to compete in today's workplace because they are ill equipped without a basic understanding of how to network, write a resume, and conduct themselves in an interview.

Barriers to Getting a Job

In this section, we will present the major mistakes that prevent job seekers from getting hired.

10- to 12-hour Work Week

For a person who is unemployed, job hunting should be a 40-hour work week. You must not burn out after a few hours to return home to wait for that "phone call." You must talk to people to get leads. Don't be surprised if you meet someone who will change your life.

Failure to Network

Networking is making and using contacts. Job hunters are not always willing to develop and pursue leads from contacts. Friends and acquaintances will give you referrals that are most effective job sources.

Canned or Poor Resumes

You must get an interview to be hired. In order to get an interview you must write a well-prepared resume and a cover letter that is original and well focused. These items are screening devices for the personnel department. You will be eliminated from consideration as an applicant if they don't indicate you are qualified and would be a good employee. This initial impression is an indication of what can be expected from you after you are hired.

Poor Interview Techniques and/or Preparation

Good physical appearance creates a positive self-image and self-respect. You must reflect a positive attitude. During the interview you must listen attentively and sell yourself by showing enthusiasm. You must communicate that you know and care about the job. Your responses must address the specific needs of the employer. It requires preparation to discover the problems of the person who has the responsibility to pick you for the position in the organization. It is most important to practice interviewing.

NETWORKING

One key element that promotes professional success is networking. Networking refers to establishing contacts with individuals who can help you succeed in your endeavors. Many jobs are attained through word-of-mouth rather than through classified advertisements. Thus, the more people you know who are in related fields, the better chances you have at being successful. How does one network? Four specific ways include colleges and professors, part-time jobs, organizations, and volunteering.

Going to college and doing well is important for many career opportunities. When you go to a four-year college or university, you should ideally pick the best college you can for your major field of study. You should distinguish yourself in that program by achieving rank in the top 10 percent of your class. You should also get to know and work with (and for) your professors and prove your abilities to them so they will be willing to recommend you when you graduate. Remember, these are important people who are well networked. You should also have one or more of these people become your mentor. Mentors are guides who help you make the right moves to be successful. Thus, do not just attend school and go home!

Another suggestion while in college is to become active in campus activities, organizations, athletics, student governments, and so on. Many organizations look for these kinds of involvement because they want well-rounded individuals working for them.

Getting a part-time job in the field you want to enter, while you are going through college, can be a great help in being successful. For example, if you are majoring in accounting, get a job with an accounting firm. The biggest and/or best would be ideal. While there, you should become the best part-time employee the company has ever had. For example, arrive at work early, leave late, and work hard. Even if your job is a low-level one to start, you will be distinguishing yourself as a unique person, and will advance and quite possibly create a good position for yourself within that company. Perhaps you will also find someone in a position above you who will become a mentor. You should also look for positions the company may not have and create that position that you feel they need and you can fill. Then go sell it to management—many people obtain very good jobs through this method.

Organizations are an excellent way to network, especially if you take leadership positions within them and become known as a "doer" who is committed and successful. Examples of organizations in which you could become active are clubs associated with your major in college. For example, if you are a finance major, join the finance club and become an officer, such as the president. Become a very active leader and do things such as bringing onto the campus successful professional people in your field to speak to your group. Get to know these people and impress them. There are also state and national organizations affiliated with your major field. For example, future teachers may want to become student members of groups such as the National Education Association and California Teachers Association.

Becoming involved in civic organizations is also a good idea. Examples are Rotary, Lions, Kiwanis, Soroptimist, American Association of University Women, and breakfast business networking clubs. In these organizations you are not only networking with successful people, but you also have the opportunity to "give back" to your community through service projects.

Volunteering is another way to "give back" to your community as well as get to know other successful people. You may want to volunteer in political campaigns, hospitals, Special Olympics, Red Cross, or United Way, for example.

In summary, networking is important to your professional success. Not only do you become acquainted with people, but you contribute to your community, expand your social skills, and build lasting friendships.

The impossible is often the untried. —*J. Goodwin*

Exploring Resumes and Cover Letters

PURPOSE

To critically analyze resumes and cover letters for their strengths and weaknesses.

PROCEDURE

In the next few pages you will view a variety of resumes and cover letters. *As individuals select one resume and one cover letter from the following pages and critique both based on the following areas.*

Resumes:

1. Does the format look appealing and balanced?

2. What words could be "stronger" or improved upon?

3. What other ways could you format this resume for greater appeal?

4. Are there any areas that could be eliminated? Is everything absolutely necessary?

Cover letters

1. Is the letter in the appropriate format?

2. What language could be stronger?

3. Does the "close" appear assertive and strong?

4. Is the letter too long or short?

5. Does the letter have a "generic feel" or a "personal feel"?

DISCUSSION

1. Pair up with other members in class and compare your critiques and suggestions.
2. Discuss the importance of the cover letter and the resume to the interview process, and brainstorm on some do's and don'ts for success in these two areas.
3. Share and discuss your ideas as a class.

Sample Cover Letter 1

East Willow Ave.
Inglewood, CA 90027
April 15, 2004

Personal Director
The Povine Company
Newport Center Dr.
Newport Beach, CA 92663

Sir:

I wish to express my interest in the position of Personnel Representative which I saw advertised in the *L.A. Times*. I fulfill all of the basic qualifications listed in the position described. I have two years of experience working in the Personnel Department at Hughes Aircraft. As Assistant to the Director of Human Resources at a large school district, I also had the opportunity to become experienced in the area of training and development. In addition to these skills, I have screened, interviewed, and referred candidates for employment in a wide variety of job classifications.

I currently hold an A.A. Degree in Business Management and will receive my B.A. in June with Personnel Administration as my major. I minored in economics and have a fine mix of academic preparation and practical experience for success in a business-related environment.

My resume details above mentioned experience as well as other skills I possess that may also be attractive to your company. I look forward to meeting with you to discuss in depth my abilities and your company's needs. I will call you in two weeks.

Thank you for your time and consideration

Gary B. Swelt

Home phone: (310) 432-1167
Bus. Phone(714) 911-7621

Enclosure

SAMPLE COVER LETTER 2

July 23, 2004

Mr. Harold E. Spring, President
Product Market, Inc.
Anywhere St.
Thistown, Iowa
52004

Dear Mr. Spring,

I am sending you with this letter my own Resume because I saw you add in the Times. I would very much like to have this job. I am working part-time in sells and would really like to move up.

In the past several years. I have worked over 175,000 hours in the sales and marketing of Stayway products.

I am contacting you because your company looks to be in need of a man with my incomparable experience to work on a full time basis. If so you may be interested in some of the things I have done.

For example, during the past year, I have singlehandedly sold over $5,000,000 worth of computer equipment and services throughout the United States. Due to these sales, I have been the number one salesman for Allied Computers for the last year.

During the last five years, I have been responsible for over $25,000,000 in retail sales for products raging from tools and hardware to sophisticated computers.

If this kind of experience would be invaluable to your company, I would love to talk with you.

Fondly,

Harrison L. Smith
Sycamore Street
Any town, Arizona 92651

SAMPLE RESUME 1

Roberta Tracy
Walnut St.
Colleyville, TX 76000
Home Phone: (817) 498-3775
Work Phone: (817) 597-9086

OBJECTIVE: A professional level position in personnel

EXPERIENCE   Over 17 years of general personnel experience in business and
SUMMARY: Industry with specialization in college recruiting.

EXPERIENCE:

1983–Present   <u>Miller-Berger Construction</u>
               Employment Representative

               Responsible for recruitment, selection and placement of all company
               employees as well as new employee orientation.
               <u>Accomplishments:</u> Designed college recruitment brochure to attract college graduates to company management positions. Designed and implemented new employee orientation.

1979–1983   <u>Colleyville Water and Power</u>
               Employment Clerk-Interviewer

               Responsible for accepting and screening applications, writing follow-up correspondence and interviewing clerical personnel.
               <u>Accomplishments:</u> Designed interview follow-up letters as well as interview appraisal sheet. Administered and scheduled typing tests. Participated in new employee orientation.

1978–1979   <u>St. Theresa's Hospital</u>
               Employment Clerk

               Responsible for accepting and filing applications and Equal Employment Opportunity cards as well as preparing and delivering weekly jobline phone message.
               <u>Accomplishments</u>: Developed efficient application filing system. Designed internal job posting format and system.

EDUCATION: A.A. Speech Communication, Austin Community College 1994
             B.A. Business, Baylor University (in progress)
MISCELLANEOUS:
Dean's Honor Roll 1993 and 1994
             Officer: Student Speech Communication Association
             Member: Personnel and Industrial Relations Association (PIRA)

Sample Resume 2

Gary B. Swelt
Portray Place
Orange, CA 92633
(714) 499-7621

CAREER OBJECTIVE

Personal Management

Personal Administration

Monitored performance evaluations
Assisted in wage and salary upgrades
Surprised clerical staff of three job classifications
Provided input into department budget
Conducted panel interviews
Recruited for various position classifications
Interviewed and referred candidates for vacant position
Coordinated generalist employment functions

Training

Performed training needs assessment
Facilitated new-employee orientation program
Conducted in-house workshop for employees on motivation
Planned in-service training

Employment

Employment Coordinator, Taco Bell, Inc., Irvine, CA 95– Present
Personnel/Training Asst., H.B.U.S.D. Huntington Beach, CA 94–95
Personnel Clerk/Receptionist, Hughes Aircraft, Torrance 90–94
Yeoman, Ship's Office, U.S. Navy, San Diego, CA 86–90

Education

B.A. Personnel Administration, California State Univ. Long Beach, 1993
A.A. Business Management, Orange Coast College 1988

Afffiliations

Toastmakers International, Club #233 Newport Beach Chapter
American Society for Personnel Administration

SAMPLE RESUME 3

Gene A. Allen

REUME
Wheat Lane
Anytown, New Jersey
80091

Date of Birth: 7/7/56
Height: 5'11"
Weight: 189
Health: Very good
Sex: Male
Marital Status: Single

EDUCATIONAL EXPEERIENCE:

High School Diploma (1974)
Seal High School
GPA: 2.0

Bachelor of Arts (1978)
Emory University, New York
Major: Business Administration
GPA: 3.0
Activities: President of AEO Fraternity
Varsity Football

Master of Science (1980)
Emory University, New York
Major: Economics
GPA:3.0

WORK EXPERIENCE:

1980 to 1988	Position:	Administrative Assistant
	Place:	Vanderbilt University, New York
	Duties:	Assisted college president with all of his duties.
1988 to Present	Position:	Executive Director, UNICEF
	Place:	Baltimore, Maryland
	Duties:	Worked with 480 employees; in charge of in-service training and coordination of 53 field offices
	Supervisor:	Dr. M.L.Singe

REFERENCES—will be furnished on request

OUTSIDE INTERESTS—racquetball, astrology, bridge, sailing, skiing, and wood working

Brainstorming for Resumes

PURPOSE

To brainstorm some ways to create effective resumes.

PROCEDURE

1. In small groups, think up as many possible suggestions for resumes as you can.
2. Brainstorm at least 20 action verbs that can be used for accomplishments. Examples include designed, presented, developed, created.
3. Get back into a large group and present your ideas to the class.

DISCUSSION

1. What types of resumes were most and least effective? Why?
2. To what extent would it be important to tailor a specific resume to a specific job?

INTERVIEW PREP KIT

Once you have been notified that you are to have an interview, it makes good sense to prepare. An interview is not a "spontaneous" event. It is a sales experience. You must use your interview time to convince the company that you are the one for the available position. Careful preparation will help you display yourself well.

Your interviewer may have a copy of your resume in advance. For some jobs, usually hourly rated, resumes are not requested. It is useful, however, to have some ready in any case. You will usually fill out an application blank in advance. Take care in filling out applications. Take all the time you need to guarantee precision and accuracy.

Once you enter the interview, pay attention to the amenities. Watch for directions about where to sit. Take the cue from the interviewer about whether you are to exchange names and shake hands. Wait for him or her to start the interview—do not blurt out how eager you are to go to work.

Dress Carefully

Do not convey messages that you do not intend to convey. A great many decisions are made about us based on the way we dress. For example, if we are wearing excessively expensive clothing to an interview, the interviewer may conclude that we tend to live beyond our means. The best advice is to dress discreetly, using quiet, semi-dark or dark colors, with little ornamentation. The clothing need not be high fashion, or even new. But it must be neat and clean, and appropriate to the occasion.

By permission, Dr. G. M. Phillips; Penn State University

Prepare Yourself with Information about the Company

Many companies provide a brochure for prospective employees. If your company does, you can get the following information from the brochure. If there is no brochure, check at your local library to find out about the company. If both of these alternatives are unavailable, feel free to ask for information at the interview.

Knowledge about company

1. Name, location, size of the company and type of business
2. Types of jobs currently available
3. Conditions under which you might work
4. Nature of the training program
5. Opportunities for education and advancement
6. Promotion policies
7. Whether there is a union
8. The fiscal history and employment stability record of the company
9. Turnover rate and prognosis for permanence
10. Whether travel or relocation is required
11. Salary offered, job description, qualifications for the position
12. Nature of the community in which the company is located
13. Employee benefits

You should be suspicious of any company that is unwilling to provide this basic information. Be careful in asking about it, however. You do not want to give the impression that #12 is more important than #3 or #5. Consider the impact of the questions on your potential future employer.

Prepare Your Remarks for the Interview

Your interviewer will use the interview to size you up to see if you are qualified, will fit into the company, and have the kind of personality they are seeking. Given that you are equally qualified with your competition, whether you are hired is at the discretion of the interviewer. Generally, people who are sloppy, inarticulate, excessively heavy, smokers, drug or alcohol users, unconcerned, and who cannot prove what they assert or "lip off" to the interviewer, do not get hired. There is no affirmative action procedure for these people. However, heavy people can reduce, sloppy people can dress neatly, and inarticulate people can learn speech skills.

There are certain types of questions that are currently illegal. If you are asked these kinds of questions, you face a moral problem. You might blow the interview if you do not answer them. If you answer them, you may answer them wrong. You always have the right to protest to the local employment service. Any employer who asks these questions may actually be trying to discriminate, but most likely they are unaware of the specifics of the law. Be careful.

Discriminatory Questions

1. Employers cannot ask you what your name was before you changed it.
2. Employers cannot inquire about your birthplace, or the birthplace of any member of your family.
3. Employers cannot ask you to disclose your ancestry or national origin.
4. Employers cannot ask for your age unless, for some reason, it is a bona fide criterion.
5. Employers cannot ask you to name your religion, the church you attend, or state the religious holidays you observe. S/he can declare the days of work required, so that you may choose not to accept the job if it violates your religious commitment.
6. Employers cannot ask about the citizenship status of anyone except you. They may ask if you are a citizen or whether you intend to become one.
7. Employers cannot ask any questions at all about your relatives. They may ask you for the name of someone to notify in case of emergency.
8. Employers cannot ask about your national origin or race.
9. Employers cannot ask questions about physical handicaps unless it is specifically relevant to the job. They can require physical examinations.
10. Employers cannot ask you to report times you were charged with felonies or misdemeanors, but they can ask you to report convictions.
11. Employers cannot ask about marital status, children, expectations for children, cohabitation, your spouse, etc. They can assert the conditions of employment and let you choose.
12. Employers cannot ask you to disclose memberships in organizations that would disclose your race, religion, or national origin.
13. Questions about sexual preference are not always illegal.
14. Employers can question you intensively about your education, job qualifications, and work experience; they may require you to take whatever examinations can be justified for the position.
15. Employers can inquire into your character, including use of drugs and alcohol, hobbies, outside activities.

Under the Buckley Amendment, you can get access to your personnel file. If you are having trouble gaining employment, you may find this useful. You can discover the kinds of invidious information that might be interfering with your ambitions.

To prepare yourself best, get a one-minute speech prepared on each of the following topics. When you do, you will have an answer to the questions most frequently asked in interviews.

1. My educational achievements in high school and college.
2. What I am interested in.
3. My skills are . . .
4. How I can be motivated to do my best work.
5. The kind of criticism that helps me most.

6. How I have demonstrated leadership.
7. My vocational goals now, five years from now, 10 years from now.
8. I am mature because. . . .
9. My past work experience has been. . . .
10. I am a creative person because . . .
11. How I can help your organization.
12. Why I am interested in your company.
13. My extracurricular activities qualify me because. . . .
14. My volunteer activities qualify me because. . . .
15. What I have learned in the past few years.
16. I have read the following books and they are about . . .
17. I read the following magazines regularly because . . .
18. How I have gotten along with my previous employers.
19. What I have learned on my previous jobs.
20. My school grades do/do not estimate my ability because. . . .
21. The kind of work I am most interested in . . .
22. I can get along well with people because . . .
23. I can demonstrate that I want to get ahead by. . . .
24. How I get along with people from various backgrounds.
25. Why I am your best choice.

Do not talk about how badly you need the job. Do not run down other candidates. Be responsive to the interviewer's questions. If you do not understand a question, ask him/her to restate it. Try to integrate your prepared remarks to meet interviewer questions. Be terse or ignore illegal questions altogether.

Employers will evaluate you on: communication skills, definitive handshake, neatness in appearance and on application and vita, promptness, responsiveness to social cues, good manners, directness in answering, economy of expression, and whether you appear organized and have your future planned. They will look for willingness to work, qualifications for the job, courtesy to past employers, interest in and knowledge about the company, desire for permanence, maturity, social awareness, decisiveness, and sense of humor. They will reject you for excessive garrulity, nonresponsiveness, flippancy, temper and arrogance, name dropping (never drop the name of a company officer on a personnel interviewer. If the job is a set-up he has already done his work). Any interviewer may reject you for any reason. It is sometimes wise to ask if you can call or write (in the event you don't get the job) and get some evaluation of your performance in the interview.

After the interview, find out how you will be notified. Do not call the company unless you are asked. If you are told to, call exactly when requested. Companies do not like to be pestered. If the company does not notify you on time, wait a discreet 24 hours and go on with your search. Companies are not always reliable, but it won't help you get a job if you tell them off about it.

JOB INTERVIEWING

DO

Have a neat, conservative appearance
Look interviewer in the eye
Appear calm and relaxed
Show interest and enthusiasm
Be assertive and tactful
Use proper English
Speak clearly and loud enough
Have specific professional plans and
    goals
Be willing to compromise
Know what salary the job generally pays
Make the most of your scholastic record
Be direct and honest
Act mature and courteous
Give interviewer a firm handshake
Treat past employers with respect
Indicate a strong desire to work
Show a sense of humor when appropriate
Know what you're talking about—
    knowledge of area and job responsi-
    bilities—give short clear answers
Show high moral standards
Do your homework—find out all you can
    about the company
Be on time for interview
Ask questions and show vitality during
    the interview. Remember, this is a
    two-way street.
Show appreciation to interviewer for
    his/her time
Keep a cool head in answering all ques-
    tions
Be prepared to answer *all* kinds of ques-
    tions—rehearse with someone. Use a
    video tape.

DON'T

Look casual, sloppy
Look at other things while talking or lis-
    tening
Fidget with anything or shift in chair
Indicate lack of interest in the company
Be overbearing or very meek
Use slang or swear words
Mumble to yourself
Appear to be just rambling around
Overemphasize money
If your record is poor, have no explana-
    tion
Make excuses or evade issues
Fool around and show poor manners
Give a limp or aggressive handshake
Condemn past employers
Say you loaf during vacations, didn't like
    school work, or indicate in any way
    that you are lazy
Act like you're shopping around or only
    want the job for a short time
Be frivolous or cynical
Give vague, indefinite, long-winded
    answers
Indicate low morals, radical views, or
    prejudices
Indicate that you know nothing about the
    company and what it does
Be late, without a *very* good reason
Be apathetic or afraid to ask questions
Forget to thank the interviewer
Get frustrated and irritated
Be unprepared—take it for granted that
    you've got it made

RESUME WORKSHEET

Before you write your resume, complete the following worksheet. If you keep this form and update it periodically, you will find creating a resume less of a chore.

Personal Information

Name:

Address:

Phone Numbers: Home:

Work:

Educational Background

Degree:

Major:

From:

Date:

Honors:

Affiliations:

Degree:

Major:

From:

Date:

Honors:

Affiliations

Degree:

Major:

From:

Date:

Honors:

Affiliations:

Outside Interests

Work Experience

Position:

Place:

Dates

Duties:

Supervisor:

Position:

Place:

Dates

Duties:

Supervisor

Position:

Place:

Dates

Duties:

Supervisor:

Professional Organizations

References

Name:

Title:

Place:

Address:

Phone Number

Name:

Title:

Place:

Address:

Phone Number

Name:

Title:

Place:

Address:

Phone Number

Ideas for the design of your resume:

REACTIONS TO CHAPTER 10

1. Using the questions found in the Interview Prep Kit, prepare yourself with information about a specific company or agency in your city. List that information here.

2. Make a list of friends, relatives, and acquaintances to be part of your network.

3. You have met a person at a party. Prepare the answer to either one of these questions: "What type of work do you do?" or "What do you intend to do with your major when you graduate from college?"

4. Make a list of the most impressive things about you.

SELECTED READINGS

Adams, <u>The Dilbert Principle</u>
Auel, <u>Clan of the Cave Bear</u>
Berne, <u>Games People Play</u>
Bronson, <u>What Should I Do With My Life?</u>
Brownmiller, <u>Against Our Will; Men, Women and Rape</u>
Burley, et al., <u>Eva Cassidy: Songbird</u>
Condon, <u>Semantics and Communication</u>
Covey, <u>The 7 Habits of Highly Effective People</u>
Dyer, <u>Pulling Your Own Strings. The Sky's the Limit</u>
Farrell, <u>Women Can't Hear What Men Don't Say</u>
Fast, <u>Body Language</u>
Fromm, <u>The Art of Loving</u>
Gordon, <u>Parent Effectiveness Training</u>
Gray, <u>Men Are From Mars, Women Are From Venus</u>
Griffin, <u>Black Like Me</u>
Hall, <u>The Silent Language. Beyond Culture</u>
Harris, <u>I'm OK. You're OK</u>
James, <u>Born to Win</u>
Jung, <u>Man and His Symbols</u>
Keller, <u>An Unknown Woman</u>
Lair, <u>I Ain't Much Baby. But I'm All I Got</u>
Maslow, <u>Toward a Psychology of Being</u>
McGraw, <u>Relationship Rescue</u>
Morris, <u>Man Watching; The Human Zoo; The Naked Ape</u>
O'Neill and O'Neill, <u>Open Marriage</u>
O'Reilly, <u>The No Spin Zone</u>
Powell, <u>Why Am I Afraid to Tell You Who I Am?</u>
Poundstone, <u>How Would You Move Mount Fiji?</u>
Rogers, <u>The World According to Mr. Rogers</u>
Smith, <u>When I Say No, I Feel Guilty</u>
Tidyman, <u>Dummy</u>
Trumbo, <u>Johnny Got His Gun</u>
Zimbardo, <u>Shyness</u>
Zukar, <u>The Seat of the Soul</u>
Zunin, <u>Contact: The First Four Minutes</u>